"Father sat at the table with the fat family Bible open at the page on which the names of his seven other children were written. He added ours, Richard and Emily, which as well as being ours were his own name and Mother's. The covers of the Bible banged, shutting us all in. The Bible says that I was born on the thirteenth day of December, 1871."

Emily Carr, *Growing Pains*

"The art of Emily Carr is exactly the same in her writing as in her pictures. It is the art of eliminating all but the essentials — the essentials for her, that is, the elements which contribute to her impression — and then setting these down in the starkest, most compressed form. She had no wish to paint, or to describe in words, the things around her as other people saw them; the camera and the phonograph could do that: it was not work for the artist. What she wanted was to study the things and the events which she felt contained material, until she had extracted that material and thrown everything else away."

B. K. Sandwell in *Saturday Night*

•

THE HOUSE OF ALL SORTS

THE HOUSE
OF ALL SORTS

EMILY CARR

CLARKE, IRWIN & COMPANY LIMITED
Toronto   **Vancouver**

Copyright, 1944

Clarke, Irwin & Company Limited

First paperback edition, 1967
Centennial Edition, 1971

ISBN   0-7720-0204-5

4 5 6   JD   76 75 74

Printed in Canada

CONTENTS

The House of All Sorts

Foundation	3
Friction	5
Sounds and Silences	8
Old Attic	9
Attic Eagles	10
Brooding and Homing	12
Space	13
First Tenant	14
Dew and Alarm Clocks	17
Money	19
Direct Action	21
Cold Sweat	22
A Tyrant and a Wedding	24
A Visitor	29
The Doll's House Couple	31
References	33
Dogs and Cats	36
Matrimony	37
Life Loves Living	39
Brides	41
Always Something	44
Mean Baby	47
Bachelors	51
Bangs and Snores	54

Zig-Zag . . . Ki-Hi	55
Blind	57
Snow	62
Arabella Jones's Home	64
Awful Partic'lar	68
Gran's Battle	70
Peach Scanties	73
Sham	75
Mrs. Pillcrest's Poems	79
Unmarried	84
Studio	87
Art and the House	91
Men Called Her Jane	96
Furniture	100
Making Musicians	104
John's Pudding	107
How Long!	110

Bobtails

Kennel	114
Punk	118
Beacon Hill	121
The Garden	123
Sunday	124
Puppy Room	126
Poison	128
Naming	130
Meg the Worker	131
Basement	133
Night	134
The Dog-Thief	135
Selling	136
Kipling	137

Lorenzo Was Registered	139
Sissy's Job	141
Min the Nurse	143
Babies	145
Distemper	148
Gertie	150
The Cousins' Bobtails	153
Blue or Red	155
Decision	158
Loo	161
Last of the Bobtails	164

To My Friends
Bill and Irene Clarke

THE HOUSE OF ALL SORTS

Foundation

THE HOUSE OF ALL SORTS could not have been quite itself in any other spot in the world than just where it stood, here, in Victoria, across James' Bay and right next to Beacon Hill Park. The house was built on part of the original property my father had chosen when he came to the new world and settled down to raise his family. This lot was my share of the old cow pasture. Father's acreage had long ago been cut into city lots. Three houses had been built in the cow yard, more in the garden and others in the lily field. The old house in which I was born was half a block away; one of my sisters still lived in it, and another in her little schoolhouse built in what had once been the family vegetable garden.

Bothers cannot be escaped by property owners and builders of houses. I got my share from the very digging of the hole for the foundation of the House of All Sorts. But the foundations of my house were not entirely of brick and cement. Underneath lay something too deep to be uprooted when they dug for the basement. The builders did not even know it was there, did not see it when they spread the cement floor. It was in my memory as much as it was in the soil. No house *could* sit it down, no house blind what my memory saw—a cow, an old white horse, three little girls in pinafores, their arms full of dolls and Canton-flannel rabbits made and stuffed with bran by an aunt, three little girls running across the pasture to play "ladies" in the shrubberies that were screened from Simcoe Street by Father's hawthorn hedge, a hedge now grown into tall trees, flowering in the month of May.

I remembered how I had poked through the then young bushes to hang over those old rotted pickets, now removed to permit the dumping of the lumber for my house. I remembered how I had said to Bigger and Middle, "Listen, girls, see if you can tell what sort of person is coming up the street by the kind of tune I blow," and I put the harmonica to my lips and puffed my cheeks. But a gentle little old lady passed, so I played very softly. She stopped and smiled over the fence at the three of us, and at the dolls and foolish, lop-eared, button-eyed rabbits.

"Eh, dearies, but how you are happy playing ladies in this sweetie wee grove!"

And now my house was built in the "sweetie wee grove," and I was not playing "lady," but was an actual landlady with tenants, not dollies, to discipline. And tenants' pianos and gramaphones were torturing my ears, as my harmonica had tortured the ears of Bigger and Middle. The little old lady had made the long pause—she would not come that way again.

Ah! little old lady, you, like cow, horse, dolls and rabbits, contributed a foundation memory to the House of All Sorts.

Friction

FRICTION quickly scraped the glamour of newness from my house—even from the start of its building. My Architect was a querulous, dictatorial man who antagonized his every workman. He had been recommended to me by an in-law; like a fool I trusted and did not investigate for myself, making enquiry of the two Victoria families he had built for since coming out from England. Always impatient, as soon as I decided to build I wanted the house immediately.

I drew up a plan and took it to the Architect asking what roughly such a building would cost. He took my plan, said it was "concise and practical"—if I would leave it with him a day or two he'd look it over and return it to me with some idea of the cost so that I could decide whether I wanted to build or not.

"A very good little plan," the man said. "But naturally I could make a suggestion or two."

In a few days he returned my drawing so violently elaborated that I did not recognize it. I said, "But this is not the house I want." He replied tartly that I would have to pay him two hundred dollars whether I accepted his plan or not because of the time he had spent mutilating it unasked! I made enquiry from the other people he had built for, finding out he had been most unsatisfactory. I was too inexperienced to fight. I knew nothing about house building; besides, I was at the time living and teaching in Vancouver. I could not afford to pay another architect as well as this one for his wretched plan. It seemed there was nothing to do but go on.

The man hated Canada and all her living. *He* was going

to show her how to build houses the English way. He would not comply with Canadian by-laws; I had endless trouble, endless expense through his ignorance and obstinacy. I made frequent trips up and down between Vancouver and Victoria. Then the man effected measles and stayed off the job for six weeks, babying himself at home, though he lived just round the corner from my half-built house.

I had hundreds of extra dollars to pay because of the man's refusal to comply with the city by-laws and the building inspectors' ripping the work out. It was a disheartening start for the House of All Sorts, but, when once I was quit of the builders and saw my way to climbing out of the hole of debt they had landed me in, I was as thrilled as a woman is over her first baby even if it is a cripple.

The big boom in Victoria property tumbled into a slump, an anxious shuddery time for every land-owner. There had been no hint of such a reverse when I began building. Houses were then badly needed. Now the houses were half of them staring blankly at each other.

Tenants were high-nosed in their choosing of apartments. The House of All Sorts was new and characterless. It had not yet found itself—and an apartment house takes longer to find itself than do individual private houses.

I had expected to occupy the Studio flat and paint there, but now the House of All Sorts could not afford a janitor. I had to be everything. Rents had lowered, taxes risen. I was barely able to scrape out a living. Whereas I had been led to believe when I started to build there would be a comfortable living, all the rentals together barely scraped out a subsistence.

The House of All Sorts was at least honest even if it was not smart. People called it quaint rather than that. It was an average house, built for average tenants. It was moderately made and moderately priced. It had some things that ultra-modern apartments do not have these days—clear views from every window, large rooms and open fire-places as well as furnace heat. Tenants could make *homes* there. Lower East and Lower West were practically semi-detached cottages.

It takes more than sweet temper to prevent a successful Landlady from earning the title of "Old Crank."

Over-awareness of people's peculiarities is an unfortunate trait for a Landlady to possess. I had it. As I approached my house from the street its grim outline seemed to slap me in the face. It was mine. Yet by paying rent others were entitled to share it and to make certain demands upon me and upon my things. I went up a long, steep stair to my door. The door opened and gulped me. I was in the stomach of the house, digesting badly in combination with the others the House of All Sorts had swallowed, mulling round in one great, heavy ache. Then along would come Christmas or the signing of the armistice, or a big freeze-up with burst pipes, an earthquake, a heat wave —some universal calamity or universal joy which jumped us all out of ourselves and cleared the atmosphere of the house like a big and bitter pill.

Sounds and Silences

SOMETIMES I rented suites furnished, sometimes un-furnished, according to the demand. Two things every tenant provided for himself—sound and silence. His own personality manufactured these, just as he stamped his imprint on every inch of his environment, placing his furniture just so, hoisting and lowering his window blinds straight or crooked. Even the boards of the floor creaked differently to each tenant's tread, walls echoed his noises individually, each one's hush was a different quiet.

Furniture is comical. It responds to humans. For some it looks its drabbest, for others it sparkles and looks, if not handsome, at any rate comfortable. And heavens! how tormenting furniture is to a guilty conscience—squeaking, squealing, scrooping! Let someone try to elude rent day or contemplate a fly-by-night. That man the furniture torments.

Old Attic

THE ATTIC was no older than the rest of the house. Yet, from the first to me it was very old, old in the sense of dearness, old as the baby you hug and call "dear old thing" is not old in years, but just in the way he has tangled himself round your heart, has become part of you so that he seems always to have existed, as far back as memory goes. That was the way with my attic. Immediately I came into the house the attic took me, just as if it had always "homed" me, became my special corner—the one place really my own. The whole house, my flat, even my own studio, was more or less public. People could track me down in any part of the house or even in the garden. Nobody ever thought of tracking me up to my attic.

I had a fine bedroom off the studio, but I kept that as a guest room, preferring to sleep in my attic. A narrow, crooked little stair in one corner of the studio climbed to a balcony, no more than a lower lip outside the attic door. If people could not find me about house or garden, they stood in the studio and shouted. Out I popped on the tiny balcony, high up on the studio wall, like a cuckoo popping out of a clock.

In the attic I could wallow in tears or in giggles,— nobody saw.

There was an outer hall and front door shared by the doll's flat and my own. If the doorbell rang while I was in my attic, I stuck my head out of the window in the gable without being seen, and called, "Who? Down in a second!"

That second gave me a chance to change my face. Those experienced in landladying told me, "Develop the 'landlady face,' my dear—not soft, not glad, not sorry, just blank."

Attic Eagles

THE SLOPE of my attic roof rose in a broad benevolent peak, poking bluntly into the sky, sinking to a four-foot wall. At one end of the gable were two long, narrow windows which allowed a good view to come into the room, a view of sea, roof tops and purple hills. Directly below the windows spread a great western maple tree, very green. Things about my place were more spready than high, myself, my house, the sheep-dogs, and Dolf, the Persian cat, whose silver fleece parted down the centre of his back and fluffed wide. Even my apple trees and lilacs grew spready.

In the wall, opposite the windows of my attic, was the room door with a tiny landing before it. Off this landing and over the studio was a dark cobwebby place, tangled with wiring, plumbing, ventilation and mystery. The plaster had oozed up through the lathing on the wrong side of the ceiling and set in bumpy furrows. I had a grim dislike of this place but the high studio ventilated through it, so the little square door had to be left ajar. I painted an Indian bear totem on this white-washed door.

On the generous slope of the attic roof I painted two Indian eagles. They were painted right on the under side of the roof shingles. Their great spread wings covered the entire ceiling of the attic. The heads of the eagles tilted upwards in bold, unafraid enquiry. I loved to lie close under these strong Indian symbols. They were only a few feet above my face as I slept in this attic bedroom. They made "strong talk" for me, as my Indian friends would say.

When, after twenty years, people bought my house and

turned it into a fine modern block, they did not require the attic, so they took away the little stair leading from the studio, they removed the door and windows, but they could not remove my eagles without tearing the roof off the house. The eagles belonged to the house for all time.

Old eagles, do you feel my memories come creeping back to you in your entombed, cobwebby darkness?

Brooding and Homing

HOUSE, I have gone to bed in your attic crying with smart and hurt as though I had been a hen under whose wing hornets had built their nest and stung me every time I quivered a feather. House, I have slept too in your attic, serene as a brooding dove.

The Indian eagles painted on the underside of the roof's shingles brooded over my head, as I brooded over the House of All Sorts. Three separate sets of souls beside my own it housed, souls for whose material comfort I was responsible. Every hen loosens up her feathers to brood over what she has hatched. Often the domestic hen is badly fooled, finds herself mothering goslings, ducks or guinea-fowl instead of good, ordinary chickens. Only the hen who "steals her nest away" can be sure whose eggs she is sitting on.

The House of All Sorts seemed to get more goslings and guinea-fowl than plain chickens. I tried to be a square old hen, but the mincing guineas and the gawky goslings tried me. The guineas peeped complainingly, the goslings waddled into all the puddles and came back to chill my skin. In no time too they outgrew my brooding squat, hoisting me clear off my feet.

You taught me, old House, that every bird wants some of her own feathers in the lining of her nest.

At first I tried to make my suites into complete homes—arranged everything as I would like it myself—but people changed it all round, discarded, substituted. It is best in a House of All Sorts to provide the necessary only and leave each woman to do her own homing.

12

Space

ROOF, WALLS, floor can pinch to hurting while they are homing you, or they can hug and enfold. Hurt enclosed is hurting doubled; to spread misery thins it. That is why pain is easier to endure out in the open. Space draws it from you. Enclosure squeezes it close.

I know I hurt my tenants sometimes—I wanted to; they hurt me! It took a long time to grind me into the texture of a landlady, to level my temperament, to make it neither all up nor all down.

The tenant always had this advantage—he could pick up and go. I could not. Fate had nailed me down hard. I appeared for the present to have no hammer-claw strong enough to pry myself loose. No, I was not nailed, I was *screwed* into the House of All Sorts, twist by twist. Every circumstance, financial, public, personal, artistic, had taken a hand in that cruel twirling of the driver. My screws were down to their heads. Each twist had demanded—"Forget you ever wanted to be an artist. Nobody wanted your art. Buckle down to being a landlady."

If only I could have landladied out in space it would not have seemed so hard. The weight of the house crushed me.

First Tenant

SHE WAS a bride just returned from honeymooning, this first tenant of mine. Already she was obviously bored with a very disagreeable husband. In her heart she knew he was not proud of her. He kept his marriage to this Canadian girl secret from his English mother.

The bride was a shocking housekeeper and dragged round all day in boudoir cap, frowsy negligée and mules—slip, slop, slip, slop. In my basement I could hear her overhead. Occasionally she hung out a grey wash, left it flapping on the line for a week, unless, for very shame, I took it in to her. "Awfully kind," she would say, "I've been meaning to bring it in these six days. Housekeeping is such a bore!" As far as I could see she did not do any. Even trees and bushes flutter the dust off, manage to do some renewing. Slip, slop—slip, slop—her aimless feet traipsed from room to room. She did not trouble to raise the lid of the garbage can, but tossed her discards out of the back door. Occasionally she dressed herself bravely and, hanging over the front gate, peered and peered. As people passed, going to Beacon Hill Park, she would stop them, saying, "Was there a thin man in grey behind you when you turned into this street?"

Astonished they asked, "Who would it be?"

"My husband—I suppose he has forgotten me again—a bachelor for so long he forgets that he has a wife. He promised to take me to the Races to-day—Oh, dear!"

Going into her flat she slammed the door and melted into negligée again.

He was a horrid man, but I too would have tried to

forget a wife like that. Negligée, bad cooking, dirty house!

They had leased my flat for six months. Three days before the fourth month was up, the man said to me casually,

"We leave here on the first."

"Your lease?" I replied.

"Lease!" He laughed in my face. "Leases are not worth their ink. Prevent a landlady from turning you out, that's all."

I consulted the lawyer who admitted that leases were all in favour of the tenant. He asked, "Who have you got there?" I told him.

"I know that outfit. Get 'em out. Make 'em go in the three days' notice they gave you. Tell them if they don't vacate on the dot they must pay another full month. Not one day over the three, mind you, or a full month's rental!"

When I told the couple what the lawyer had said they were very angry, declaring that they could not move in three days' time, but that they would not pay for overtime.

"All right," I said. "Then the lawyer . . ."

They knew the lawyer personally and started to pack violently.

The bride and groom had furnished their own flat— garish newness, heavily varnished, no nearer to being their own than one down payment, less near, in fact, as the instalments were overdue. Store vans came and took the furniture back. The woman left in a cab with a couple of suitcases. The forwarding address she left was that of her mother's home. The man left a separate forwarding address. His was a hotel.

To describe the cleaning of that flat would be impossible. As a parting niceness the woman hurled a pot of soup—meat, vegetables and grease—down the kitchen sink. She said, "You hurried our moving," and shrugged.

The soup required a plumber.

This first tenant nearly discouraged me with landladying. I consulted an experienced person. She said, "In time you will learn to make yourself hard, hard!"

Dew and Alarm Clocks

POETICAL extravagance over "pearly dew and daybreak" does not ring true when that most infernal of inventions, the alarm clock, wrenches you from sleep, rips a startled heart from your middle and tosses it on to an angry tongue, to make ugly splutterings not complimentary to the new morning; down upon you spills cold shiveriness—a new day's responsibilities have come.

To part from pillow and blanket is like bidding goodbye to all your relatives suddenly smitten with plague.

The attic window gaped into empty black. No moon, no sun, no street lamps. Trees, houses, telephone poles muddled together and out in that muddle of blank perhaps one or two half-hearted kitchen lights morosely blinking. Sun had not begun.

The long outside stair, from flat to basement, never creaked so loudly as just before dawn. No matter how I tiptoed, every tread snapped, "Ik!"

Punk, the house dog, walked beside me step by step, too sleepy to bounce.

Flashlights had not been invented. My arms threshed the black of the basement passage for the light bulb. Cold and grim sat that malevolent brute the furnace, greedy, bottomless—its grate bars clenched over clinkers which no shaker could dislodge. I was obliged to thrust head and shoulders through the furnace door. I loathed its black, the smell of soot. I was sure one day I should stick. I pictured the humiliation of being hauled out by the shoes. Could I ever again be a firm dignified landlady after being pulled like that from a furnace mouth!

I could hear tenants still sleeping—the house must be warm for them to wake to. . . .

"Woo, Woo!" A tiny black hand drew the monkey's box curtain back. "Woo, Woo!" A little black face enveloped in yawn peeped out. One leg stretched, then the other. "Woo." She crept from her box to feel if her special pipe was warm, patted approvingly, flattened her tummy to the heat. The cat came, shaking sleep out of her fur. Crackle, crackle!—the fire was burning. Basement windows were now squares of blue-grey dawn.

Carrying a bucket of ashes in each hand I went into the garden, feeling like an anchor dropped overboard. Everything was so coldly wet, I so heavy. Dawn was warming the eastern sky just a little. The Bobbies were champing for liberty. They had heard my step. The warmth of their loving did for the garden what the furnace was doing for the house.

Circled by a whirl of dogs I began to live the day.

We raced for Beacon Hill, pausing when we reached its top. From here I could see my house chimney—mine. There *is* possessive joy, and anyway the alarm clock would not rouse me from sleep for another twenty-three hours—might as well be happy!

Up came the sun, and drank the dew.

Money

FROM THE moment key and rent exchanged hands a subtle change took place in the attitude of renter towards owner.

The tenant was obviously anxious to get you out, once the flat was hers. She might have known, silly thing, that you wanted to be out—before she began to re-arrange things.

Bump, bump, bump! It would never do to let a landlady think her taste and arrangement were yours. Particularly women with husbands made it their business to have the man exchange every piece of furniture with every other. When they left you had to get some one to move them all back into place. When once they had paid and called it "*my* flat" they were always asking for this or that additional furniture or privilege.

There was the tenant who came singing up my long stair and handed in the rent with a pleasant smile. It was folded in a clean envelope so that the raw money was not handled between you. You felt him satisfied with his money's worth. Perhaps he did change his furniture about, just a little, but only enough to make it home him. Every hen likes to scrape the straw around her nest, making it different from every other hen's. There was the pompous person who came holding a roll of bills patronizingly as if he were handing you a tip. There was the stingy one, parting hardly with his cash, fishing the hot tarnished silver and dirty bills from the depths of a trouser pocket and counting them lingeringly, grudgingly, into your palm. There was the rent dodger who always forgot rent date. There was every kind of payer. But most renters seemed to regard rent as an unfairness—was not the earth the Lord's? Just so, but who pays the taxes?

Direct Action

OUR DISTRICT was much too genteel to settle disagreements by a black eye or vituperation. Troubles were rushed upstairs to the landlady. I wished my tenants would emulate my gas stove. In proud metallic lettering she proclaimed herself "Direct action" and lived up to it.

How bothersome it was having Mrs. Lemoyne mince up my stair to inform on Mrs. FitzJohn; having to run down the long stair, round the house and carry the complaint to Mrs. FitzJohn, take the retort back to Mrs. Lemoyne and return the ultimatum—upping and downing until I was tired! Then, often, to find that there was no trouble between the two ladies at all. The whole affair was a fix-up, to convey some veiled complaint against my house or against me, to have the complainer send a sweet message to the complained-of: "Don't give the matter another thought, my dear. It is really of no consequence at all," and from my window see the ladies smiling, whispering, nodding in the direction of my flat. I would have liked better an honest pig-sow who projected her great grunt from the depths of her pen right into one's face.

My sisters, who lived round the corner from the House of All Sorts, watched my landladying with disapproval, always siding with the tenant and considering my "grunt" similes most unrefined. But they did not have to be landladies.

Cold Sweat

HIS HAND trembled—so did his voice.

"You will leave the door of your flat unlocked tonight? So that I could reach the 'phone?"

"Certainly."

He went to the door, stood there, clinging to the knob as if he must hold on to something.

"Beautiful night," he said and all the while he was turning up his coat collar because of the storming rain outside. He went into the night. I closed the door; the knob was wet with the sweat of his hand.

Bump, bump, bump, and a curse. I ran out and looked over the rail. He was rubbing his shins.

"That pesky cat—I trod on her—" he cursed again. He loved that cat. I heard him for half an hour calling among the wet bushes. "Puss, Puss, poor Puss." Maybe that mother cat knew his mind needed to be kept busy and was hiding.

I was just turning in when he came again.

"She's all right."

"You have had word? I am so glad—"

"The cat, I mean," he said, glowering at me. "She was not hurt when I trod on her—shan't sleep tonight—not one wink, but if I should not hear your 'phone—would you call me?—leave your window open so I shall hear the ring?"

"All right, I'll call you; I am sure to hear if you don't."

"Thanks, awfully."

The telephone did not ring. In the morning he looked worse.

He came up and sat by the 'phone, scowling at the

instrument as if it were to blame. At last he found courage to ring the hospital. After a terse sentence or two he slammed the receiver down and sat staring.

"That your porridge burning?"

"Yes!" He rushed down the stair, and returned immediately with the black, smoking pot in his hand.

"If it were not Sunday I'd go to the office—hang! I'll go anyhow."

"Better stay near the 'phone. Why not a hot bath?"

"Splendid idea. But—the 'phone?"

"I'll be here."

No sooner was he in the tub than the message came.

"You are wanted on the 'phone." I shouted through two doors.

"Take it." He sounded as if he were drowning.

I was down again in a moment. "A boy—both doing well." Dead stillness.

By and by I went down. He was skimming the cream off the milk jug into the cat's dish. The hair stuck damp on his forehead, his cheeks were wet.

"Thank God I was in the tub! I could not have stood it—I should never have thought of asking how she—*they* —were." Realization of the plural clicked a switch that lit up his whole being.

A Tyrant and a Wedding

SHE CAME from the prairie, a vast woman with a rolling gait, too much fat, too little wind, only one eye.

She stood at the bottom of the long stair and bribed a child to tell me she was there. Her husband sat on the verandah rail leaning forward on his stick, her great shapeless hand steadying him. This lean, peevish man had no more substance than a suit on a hanger. A clerical collar cut the mean face from the empty clothes.

The old lady's free hand rolled towards the man. "This," she said, "is the Reverend Daniel Pendergast. I am Mrs. Pendergast. We came about the flat."

The usual rigmarole—rental—comfortable beds—hot water . . . They moved in immediately.

I despised the Reverend Pendergast more every day. His heart was mean as well as sick. He drove the old lady without mercy by night and by day. She did his bidding with patient, adoring gasps. He flung his stick angrily at every living thing, be it wife, beast or bird—everything angered him. Then he screamed for his wife to pick up his stick—retrieve it for him like a dog. She must share his insomnia too by reading to him most of the night; that made the tears pour out of the seeing and the unseeing eye all the next day. Her cheeks were always wet with eye-drips.

I was sorry for the old lady. I liked her and did all I could to help her in every way except in petting the parson. She piled all the comforts, all the tidbits, on him. When I took her flowers and fruit from my garden, it was he that always got them, though I said, most pointedly, "For *you,*

Mrs. Pendergast," and hissed the "s's" as loud as I could.

She would beg me, "Do come in and talk to 'Parson'; he loves to see a fresh face."

Sometimes, to please her, I sat just a few minutes by the sour creature.

One morning when I came down my stair she moaned through the crack of the door, "Come to me."

"What is the matter?" I said. She looked dreadful.

"I fell into the coal-bin last night. I could not get up. My foot was wedged between the wall and the step."

"Why did you not call to me?"

"I was afraid it would disturb the Parson. I got up after a while but the pain of getting up and down in the night to do for my husband was *dreadful* torture."

"And he let you do it?"

"I did not tell him I was hurt. His milk must be heated —he must be read to when he does not sleep."

"He is a selfish beast," I said. She was too deaf, besides hurting too much, to hear me.

When I had helped to fix her broken knees and back, I stalked into the living-room where the Reverend Pendergast lay on a couch.

"Mrs. Pendergast has had a very bad fall. She can scarcely move for pain."

"Clumsy woman! She is always falling down," he said indifferently.

I can't think why I did not hit him. I came out and banged the door after me loudly, hoping his heart would jump right out of his body. I knew he hated slams.

There was an outbreak of caterwaulings. The neighbourhood was much disturbed. The cats were strays— miserable wild kittens born when their owners went camping and never belonging to anyone.

The tenants put missiles on all window ledges to hurl during the night. In the morning I took a basket and gathered them up and took them to the tenants' doors so that each could pick out his own shoes, hairbrushes, pokers and

scent bottles. Parson Pendergast threw everything portable
at the cats. The old lady was very much upset at his being
so disturbed. At last, with care and great patience, I en-
ticed the cats into my basement, caught them and had
them mercifully destroyed.

When I told the Pendergasts, the Parson gave a cruel,
horrible laugh. "I crushed a cat with a plank once—beat
the life out of her, just for meowing in our kitchen—threw
her into the bush for dead; a week later she crawled home
—regular jelly of a cat." He sniggered.

"You—a parson—you did that? You cruel beast! To do
such a filthy thing!"

Mrs. Pendergast gasped. I bounced away.

I could not go near the monster after that. I used to help
the old lady just the same, but I would not go near the
Reverend Pendergast.

One day, I found her crying.

"What is it?"

"Our daughter—is going to be married."

"Why should she not?"

"He is not the kind of man the Parson wishes his daughter to marry. Besides they are going to be married by a J.P.
They will not wait for father. There is not another parson
in the vicinity."

The old lady was very distressed indeed.

"Tell your daughter to come here to be married. I will
put her up and help you out with things."

The old lady was delighted. The tears stopped trickling
out of her good eye and her bad eye too.

We got a wire off to the girl and then we began to bake
and get the flat in order.

The Parson insisted it should be a church wedding—
everything in the best ecclesiastical style, with the bishop
officiating. The girl would be two days with her parents
before the ceremony. She was to have my spare room.
However, the young man came too, so she had the couch

in her mother's sitting room. They sent him upstairs without so much as asking if they might.

I was helping Mrs. Pendergast finish the washing-up when the young couple arrived. Mrs. Pendergast went to the door. She did not bring them out where I was, but, keeping her daughter in the other room, she called out some orders to me as if I had been her servant. I finished and went away; I began to see that the old lady was a snob. She did not think me the equal of her daughter because I was a landlady.

It was very late when the mother and daughter brought the young man upstairs to my flat to show him his room. They had to pass through my studio. From my bedroom up in the attic I could look right down into the studio. My door was ajar. There was enough light from the hall to show them the way, but the girl climbed on a chair and turned all the studio lights up full. The three then stood looking around at everything, ridiculed me, made fun of my pictures. They whispered, grimaced and pointed. They jeered, mimicked, playacted me. I saw my own silly self bouncing round my own studio in the person of the old lady I had tried to help. When they had giggled enough, they showed the young man his room and the women went away.

I was working in my garden next morning when the woman and the girl came down the path. I did not look up or stop digging.

"This is my daughter . . . . You have not met, I think."

I looked straight at them, and said, "I saw you when you were in my studio last night."

The mother and daughter turned red and foolish looking; they began to talk hard.

The wedding was in the Cathedral; the old man gave his daughter away with great pomp. The other witness was a stupid man. I was paired with him. We went for a drive after the ceremony.

I had to go to the wedding breakfast because I had promised to help the old lady; I hated eating their food. The bride ordered me around and put on a great many airs.

The couple left for the boat. Mrs. Pendergast and I cleared up. We did not talk much as we worked. We were tired.

Soon the doctor said the Reverend Daniel Pendergast could go home to the prairies again because his heart was healed. I was glad when the cab rolled down the street carrying the cruel, emaciated Reverend and the one-eyed ingrate away from my house—I was glad I did not have to be their landlady any more.

A Visitor

DEATH had been snooping round for a week. Everyone in the house knew how close he was. The one he wanted lay in my spare room but she was neither here nor there. She was beyond our reach, deaf to our voices.

The sun and spring air came into her room—a soft-coloured, contented room. The new green of spring was close outside the windows. The smell of wall-flower and sweet alyssum rose from the garden, and the inexpressible freshness of the daffodils.

The one tossing on the bed had been a visitor in my house for but a short time. Death made his appointment with her there. The meeting was not hateful—it was beautiful and welcome to her.

People in the house moved quietly. Human voices were tuned so low that the voices of inanimate things—shutting of doors, clicks of light switches, crackling of fires—swelled to importance. Clocks ticked off the solemn moments as loudly as their works would let them.

Death came while she slept. He touched her, she sighed and let go.

We picked the wall-flowers and the daffodils, and brought them to her, close. There was the same still radiance about them as about her. Every bit of her was happy. The smile soaked over her forehead, eyelids and lips—more than a smile—a glad, silent expression.

Lots of people had loved her; they came to put flowers near and to say goodbye. They came out of her room with quiet, uncrying eyes, stood a moment by the fire in the studio, looking deep into it, and then they went away. We could not be sad for her.

The coffin was taken into the studio. One end rested on the big table which was heaped with flowers. The keen air came in through the east windows. Outside there was a row of tall poplars, gold with young spring.

Her smile—the flowers—quiet—possessed the whole house.

A faint subtle change came over her face. She was asking to be hidden away.

A parson came in his mournful black. He had a low, sad voice—while he was talking we cried.

They took her down the long stairs. The undertakers grumbled about the corners. They put her in the waiting hearse and took her away.

The house went back to normal, but now it was a mature place. It had known birth, marriage and death, yet it had been built for but one short year.

The Doll's House Couple

IT WAS made for them, as surely as they were made for each other. I knew it as soon as I saw the young pair standing at my door. They knew it too the moment I opened the door of the Doll's House. His eyes said things into hers, and her eyes said things into his. First their tongues said nothing, and then simultaneously, "It's ours!" The key hopped into the man's pocket and the rent hopped into mine.

One outer door was common to their flat and to mine. Every time I came in and out passing their door I could hear them chatting and laughing. Their happiness bubbled through. Sometimes she was singing and he was whistling. They must do something, they were so happy.

At five o'clock each evening his high spirits tossed his body right up the stair—there she was peeping over the rail, or hiding behind the door waiting to pounce on the tragedy written all over him because he had not found her smiling face hanging over the verandah rail. She pulled him into the Doll's House, told him all about her day—heard all about his.

She tidied the flat all day and he untidied it all night. He was such a big "baby-man," she a mother-girl who had to take care of him; she had always mothered a big family of brothers. They had taught her the strangeness of men, but she made more allowance for the shortcomings of her man than she had done for the shortcomings of her brothers.

I was making my garden when they came to live in my house. They would come rushing down the stair, he to seize my spade, she to play the hose so that I could sit and rest a little. They shared their jokes and giggles with me.

When at dusk, aching, tired, I climbed to my flat, on my table was a napkined plate with a little surprise whose odor was twin to that of the supper in the Doll's House.

Sometimes, when my inexperience was harried by Lower East or Lower West, when things were bothersome, difficult, so that I was just hating being a landlady, she would pop a merry joke or run an arm round me, or he would say, "Shall I fix that leak?—put up that shelf?"

Oh, they were like sunshine pouring upon things, still immature and hard by reason of their greenness. Other tenants came and went leaving no print of themselves behind—that happy couple left the memory of their joyousness in every corner. When, after they were gone, I went into the Doll's House emptiness, I felt their laughing warmth still there.

References

EXPERIENCE taught me to beware of people who were glib with references. I never asked a reference. I found that only villains offered them.

There was a certain Mrs. Panquist. The woman had a position in a very reputable office. Her husband was employed in another. Her relatives were people of position, respected citizens. She gave me this voluntary information when she came to look at the flat.

"It suits me," she said. "I will bring my husband to see it before deciding."

Later she rang up to say he was not coming to see it. They had decided to take the flat and would move in early the next morning. She would bring her things before business hours. Furthermore she asked that I prepare an extra room I had below for her maid. To do this I had to buy some new furniture.

She did not come or send her things next morning; all day there was no word of her. I had the new furniture bought and everything ready.

Late in the evening she arrived very tired and sour.

She snatched the key out of my hand.

"It is usual to exchange the rent for the key," I said knowing this was war-time and that there were some very shady fly-by-nights going from one apartment house to another.

"I am too tired to bother about rent tonight!" she snapped. "I will come up with it in the morning before I go to work."

Again she failed to keep her promise. I asked her for the

rent several times but she always put me off. Finally she said rudely, "I am not going to pay; my husband can."

I went to the man, who was most insolent, saying, "My wife took the flat; let her pay."

"Come," I said. "Time is going on, one or the other of you must pay." I pointed to the notice on the kitchen door "RENTS IN ADVANCE." He laughed in my face. "Bosh!" he said. "We don't pay till we are ready."

I began to make enquiries about the couple, not from those people whose names they had given as reference, but from their former landlady. Their record was shocking. They had rented from a war widow, destroyed her place, and gone off owing her a lot of money.

Both of the Panquists had jobs; they could pay and I was not going to get caught as the war widow had been.

I consulted the law—was turned over to the Sheriff.

"Any furniture of their own?"

"Only a couple of suitcases."

"Not enough value to cover the rental they owe?"

"No."

"This is what you are to do. Watch—when you see them go out take a pass key, go in and fasten up the flat so that they cannot get in until the rental is paid."

"Oh, I'm scared; the man is such a big powerful bully!"

"You asked me for advice. Take it. If there is any trouble call the police."

I carried out the Sheriff's orders, trembling.

The Panquists had a baby and a most objectionable nursemaid. She was the first to come home, bringing the child.

I was in my garden. She screamed, "The door is locked. I can't get in!"

"Take the child to the room I prepared for you." (The woman had decided she did not want it after I had bought furniture and prepared the room.) I took down milk and biscuits for the child. "When your mistress has paid the rent the door will be opened," I said. The maid bounced off and shortly returned with the woman, who stood over me in a furious passion.

"Open that door! You hear—open that door!"

"When the rent is paid. You refuse, your husband refuses. The flat is not yours till you pay. I am acting under police orders."

"I'll teach you," she said, livid with fury, and turned, rushing headlong; she had seen her husband coming.

He was a huge man and had a cruel face. His mouth was square and aggressive; out of it came foul oaths. He looked a fiend glowering at me and clenching his fists.

"You—(he called me a vile name)! Open or I will break the door in!" He braced his shoulder against it and raised his great fists. I was just another woman to be bullied, got the better of, frightened.

I ran to the 'phone. The police came. The man stood back, his hands dropping to his sides.

"What do you want me to do?" said the officer.

"Get them out. I won't house such people. They got away with it in their last place, not here."

I was brave now though I shook.

"The town is full of such," said the officer. "House owners are having a bad time. Scum of the earth squeezing into the shoes of honest men gone overseas. How much do they owe?"

I told him.

He went to the man and the woman who were snarling angrily at one another.

"Pay what you owe and get out."

"No money on me," said the man, "my wife took the flat."

"One of you must," said the officer.

"Shell out," the man told the woman brutally.

She gave him a look black with hatred, took money from her purse and flung it at me. My faith in proffered references was dead.

Dogs and Cats

AT FIRST, anxious to make people feel at home, happy in my house, I permitted the keeping of a dog or a cat, and I endured babies.

My Old English Bobtail Sheep-dogs lived in kennels beyond the foot of my garden. They had play fields. The tenants never came in contact with the dogs other than seeing them as we passed up the paved way in and out for our run in Beacon Hill Park. One old sheep-dog was always in the house with me, always at my heels. He was never permitted to go into any flat but mine. There was, too, my great silver Persian cat, Adolphus. He also was very exclusive. People admired him enormously but the cat ignored them all.

I enjoyed my own animals so thoroughly that when a tenant asked, "May I keep a dog or a cat?" I replied, "Yes, if you look after it. There are vacant lots all round and there is Beacon Hill Park to run the animal in."

But no, people were too lazy to be bothered. They simply opened their own door and shoved the creature into the narrow strip of front garden, let him bury his bones and make the lawn impossible. Always it was the landlady who had to do the tidying up. I got tired of it. Anyone should be willing to tend his creature if he has any affection for it. They managed cats even worse, these so-called "animal lovers." Stealthily at night a basement window would open, a tenant's cat be pushed through. The coal pile became impossible. I was obliged to ban all animals other than a canary bird, although I would far rather have banned humans and catered to creatures.

Matrimony

I HAD NEVER before had the opportunity of observing the close-up of married life. My parents died when I was young. We four spinster sisters lived on in the old home. My girlhood friends who married went to live in other cities. I did not know what "till-death-do-us-part" did to them.

Every couple took it differently of course, but I discovered I could place "Marrieds" in three general groupings—the happy, the indifferent, and the scrappy.

My flat being at the back of the house I overlooked no tenant nor did I see their comings and goings. The walls were as soundproof as those of most apartments, only voice murmurs came through them, not words. No secrets were let out. I neither saw nor heard, but I could *feel* in wordless sounds and in silences; through the floor when I went into my basement to tend the furnace I heard the crackle of the man's newspaper turning and turning—the creak of the woman's rocker.

There are qualities of sound and qualities of silence. When the sounds were made only by inanimate things, you knew that couple were the indifferent type. When you heard terse jagged little huddles of words, those were the snappers! If there was a continuous rumbling of conversation, contented as the singing of a tea kettle or the purring of a cat, you knew that couple had married happily. There was the way they came to pay the rent too, or ask a small favour, or project a little grumble. The happily married ones spared each other; the wife asked or grumbled for the husband, the husband for the wife.

Snappy couples tore up my stairs, so eager to "snap their snaps" that they often found themselves abreast of each other anxious to be first!

It was immaterial whether the man or the woman of the indifferent pair came. They handed in the rent grudgingly and went away without comment. I liked them the least.

Life Loves Living

THERE were four western maple trees growing in the lot upon which I built my house. Two were in the strip of front lawn, clear of foundations, but when the builders came to overhead wiring they found one of the trees interfered. The line-men cut it down. The other front-lawn maple was a strong, handsome tree. I circled her roots with rock and filled in new earth. The tree throve and branched so heavily that the windows of Lower West and the Doll's Flat were darkened. Experts with saws and ladders came and lopped off the lower branches. This sent the tree's growth rushing violently to her head in a lush overhanging which umbrellaed the House of All Sorts. She was lovely in spring and summer, but when fall came her leaves moulted into the gutters and heaped in piles on the roof, rotting the cedar shingles. It put me to endless expense of having roof-men, gutter-men and tree-trimmers. At last I gave the grim order, "Cut her down."

It is horrible to see live beauty that has taken years to mature and at last has reached its prime hacked down, uprooted.

The other two maple trees had stood right on the spot where my house was to be built. The builders had been obliged to saw them to within three or four feet of the ground. Both trees' roots were in that part underneath the house which was not to be cemented; it would always be an earthy, dark place. The maple stumps were left in the ground. One died soon. The other clung furiously to life, her sap refused to dry up; grimly she determined to go on living.

The cement basement was full of light and air, but light and air were walled away from that other part, which was low. I could not stand there upright; there was but one small square of window in the far corner. The old maple stump shot sickly pink switches from her roots, new switches every year. They crept yearningly toward the little square of window. Robbed of moisture, light and air, the maple still remembered spring and pushed watery sap along her pale sprouts, which came limper and limper each year until they were hardly able to support the weight of a ghastly droop of leaves having little more substance than cobwebs.

But the old maple stump would not give up. It seemed no living thing in the House of All Sorts had less to live for than that old western maple, yet she clung to life's last shred—she loved living.

Brides

LOWER EAST and Lower West were both rented to brides.

The brides sat in their living-rooms with only a wall dividing; they looked out at the same view. They did not know each other.

In the East flat, the young husband was trying to accommodate himself to a difficult and neurotic wife.

In the West flat a middle-aged groom was trying to slow a bright young girl down to his dullness. The girl drooped, was home-sick, in spite of all the pretty things he gave her and the smart hats she made for herself (she had been a milliner in New York before she married the middle-aged man). It was freedom she thought she was marrying— freedom from the drudgery of bread-and-butter-earning. When he dangled a "home of her own" before her eyes, she married him and was numbed; now came the pins and needles of awaking.

I had known the other bride since she was a child. When I welcomed her into my house, she chilled as if to remind me that she was a popular young bride—I a landlady; I took the hint. I had put the best I had into her flat, but she scornfully tossed my things into her woodshed, replacing them with things of her own. The rain came, and spoiled my things. When I asked her to hand back what she did not want, so that I might store them safely, she was very insulting, as if my things were beyond contempt or hurting.

The little New York bride was very, very lonely, with her dull, heavy husband. She came up to my flat on any excuse whatever. One day she cried and told me about it.

She said that she knew no one. "The girl next door is a bride too; she's smart; she has lots of friends. I see them come and go. Oh, I do wish I knew her." Then she said, "You know her; couldn't you introduce me? Please!"

"I have known her since she was a child, but I could not introduce you to each other."

"Why?"

"It is not my place to introduce tenants. People make opportunities of speaking to each other if they are neighbours, but they would resent being compelled by their landlady to know each other."

"But you have known this girl since she was little—couldn't you? I have no friends at all. Please, please."

"Listen, it would not make you happy. She is a snob."

I would not subject this unhappy, ill-bred, little bride, with her ultra clothes worn wrong, her overdone make-up and her slangy talk, to the snubs of the stuck-up bride next door.

"You'll come and see me, won't you? Come often—he is out so much."

"I will come when I can."

She went slowly down to her empty flat, this lonely little bride who had sold her pretty face for laziness and a home.

Next day she ran up, all excitement.

"My opportunity came! The postman asked me to deliver a registered letter, because my neighbour was out; you are all wrong, she is lovely. I expect we shall see a lot of each other now. I am so happy."

She flew down-stairs, hugging her joy.

I missed her for some days. I went to see if she were ill, found her crumpled into a little heap on the sofa. She had red eyes.

"Hello! Something wrong?"

She gulped hard. "It is as you said—she is a snob. We met in the street. They saw me coming. When I was close they looked the other way and talked hard. Her husband did not even raise his hat!"

"Perhaps they did not see it was you."

"They could not help seeing—not if they'd been as blind as new kittens. I spoke before I saw how they felt," she sobbed.

"Pouf! Would I care? She is not worth a cry! What pretty hats you make!"

She had been working on one—it lay on the table half finished.

"You like them? I make them all myself. I was a milliner in New York—head of all the girls. They gave me big pay because I had knack in designing—big fine store it was too!"

"Here you are crying because a snob who couldn't make one 'frump's bow' did not speak to you! Come, let's go into the garden and play with the pups."

She was soon tumbling with them on the lawn, kind whole-hearted clumsy pups, much more her type than the next-door bride.

Always Something

SHE WAS so young, so pretty, so charming! But when it came to a matter of shrewd bargaining, you couldn't beat her. Her squeezing of the other fellow's price was clever—she could have wrung juice from a raw quince. Her big husband was entirely dominated by his tall, slender wife; he admired her methods enormously. Sometimes he found it embarrassing to look into the face of the "squeezed." While she was crumbling down my rent, he turned his back, looking out of the window, but I saw that his big ears were red and that they twitched.

It was the Doll's Flat she bargained for, which seemed ridiculous seeing that he was so large, she so tall, and the Doll's Flat so little.

"Won't it be rather squeezy?" I suggested.

"My husband is used to ship cabins. For myself I like economy."

She was an extremely neat, orderly person, kept the Doll's Flat like a Doll's Flat—no bottles, no laundry, no garbage troubles, as one had with so many tenants. She made the place attractive.

She entertained a bit and told me all the nice things people said about her flat.

"If only I had 'such and such a rug' or 'such and such a curtain' it would be perfect!" and she wheedled till I got it for her. But these added charms to make her flat *perfect* always came out of my pocket, never out of hers.

I had a white cat with three snowball kittens who had eyes like forget-me-nots. When the tall, slim wife was entertaining, she borrowed my "cat family," tied blue ribbons round their necks. Cuddled on a cushion in a basket they amused and delighted her guests—inexpensive entertainment. Flowers were always to be had out of my garden for the picking.

"If only toasted buns grew on the trees!" She liked toasted buns for her tea parties—the day-before's were half-price and toasted better. . . . I heard her on my 'phone.

"Not deliver five cents' worth! Why should I buy more when I don't require them?" Down slammed the receiver and she turned to me.

"They do not deserve one's custom! I shall have to walk to town: it is not worth paying a twelve-cent carfare to fetch five cents' worth of stale buns!"

I swore at the beginning of each month I would buy nothing new for her, but before the month was out I always had, and wanted to kick myself for a weak fool. I liked her in spite of her meanness.

She was proud of her husband's looks; he wore his navy lieutenant's clothes smartly.

"Ralph, you need a new uniform."—He ordered it. "How much is the tailor charging? . . . Ridiculous!"

"He is the best tailor in town, my dear."

"Leave him to me."

The next day she came home from town. "I've cut that tailor's price in half!"

"What a clever wife!" But the lieutenant went red. He took advantage of her bargaining but he shivered at her boasting in front of me about it.

She did hate to pay a doctor. She had been a nurse before she married; she knew most of the doctors in town. It was wonderful how she could nurse along an ailment till someone in the house fell sick, then she just "happened to be coming in the gate" as the doctor went out. He would stop for a word with the pretty thing.

"How are you?"

Out came tongue and all her saved-up ailments. She ran

45

down to the druggist's to fill the prescription, to shop a little. Butcher, grocer always added a bit of suet, or a bone, or maybe she spotted a cracked egg, had it thrown in with her dozen. They *loved* doing it for her, everybody fell before her wheedle.

"I am going to stay with you forever," she had said as an inducement to make me lower the rent and buy this or that for her flat. Then, "The very smartest apartment block in town—Ralph always fancied it, but it was too expensive for us. But—only one room, a bachelor suite—the man is sub-letting at *half* its usual price, furniture thrown in. He will be away one year. Wonderful for us! Such a bargain, isn't it my dear?"

"One room!"

"But, the block is so smart: such a bargain!"

They went to their bargain room. A professor and his wife moved into my Doll's Flat. They were as lavishly open-handed as the others had been stingy. The professor was writing a book. He had a talkative wife whom he adored, but though he loved her tremendously, he could not get on with his book because of her chattering. He just picked her up, opened my door, popped her in.

"There! chatter, dear, all you like." He turned the key on his peace—what about mine? I pulled the dust-sheet over my canvas. Landlady's sighs are heavy—is it not enough to give shelter, warmth, furniture? Must a landlady give herself too?

Mean Baby

THE BABY had straight honey-coloured hair, pale eyes, puckered brow, pouting mouth, and a yell, a sheer, bad-tempered, angry yell which she used for no other reason than to make herself thoroughly unpleasant. Bodily she was a healthy child.

Her family brought her to my house suddenly because the whole lot of them had come down with measles while staying in a boarding-house nearby. The other boarders got panicky and asked them to go! Early in the morning the mother came to me, very fussed. Lower West was empty and measles being a temporary complaint, I let the woman have the flat.

When the taxi load of spotty children drove up to my door I was hustling to warm up the beds and make up extras. Some of the children sat limp and mute waiting, while others whimpered fretfully. The infant, a lumpy child of un-walking, un-talking age, was the only one who had not got measles. The mother set the child on the floor while she went to fetch the sick, spotty miseries from the cab. The infant's head, as it were, split in two—eyes, cheeks, brow retired, all became mouth, and out of the mouth poured a roar the equal of Niagara Falls.

The lady in the Doll's Flat above stuck her head out of the window and looked down. "Measles," I warned, and she drew her own and her small son's head back, closed her windows and locked her door.

The measles took their course under a doctor and a trained nurse. I ran up and down the stairs with jellies and gruel. Night and day the baby cried. The House of All Sorts supposed she was sickening for measles and endured it as best they could. The baby did not get measles. After fumigation and quarantine were over and nothing ailed the child we had the Doctor's word as assurance that it was only a cranky, mean temper that was keeping us awake all night. The tenants began coming to me with complaints, and I had to go down and talk to the mother.

I said, "No one in the house can sleep for the child's crying, something will have to be done. I cannot blame my tenants for threatening to go and I cannot afford to lose them." The woman was all syrupy enthusing over the soups and jellies I had sent the measles; but she suddenly realized that I was in earnest and that my patience for my household's rest was at an end.

If only I could have gone down to the mother in the middle of the night when we were all peevish for sleep, it would have been different, but, with the child sitting for the moment angel-like in her mother's lap, it was not easy to proceed. I looked out the window. Near the front gate I saw the child's pram drawn up dishevelled from her morning nap. What my tenants resented most was not that the child kept the whole household awake at night but that the mother put her baby to sleep most of the day in the garden, close by the gate through which people came and went to the house. After listening to her yelling all night every one was incensed to be told in the daytime, "Hush, hush! my baby is asleep: don't wake her." The mother pounced upon the little boy upstairs, upon baker, postman, milkman, visitors; every one was now afraid to come near our house; people began to shun us. I looked at the disordered pram and took courage.

"Would you please let the baby take her day naps on the back verandah; she would be quiet there and not interfere with our coming and going."

"My baby on the back porch! Certainly not!"

"Why does the child cry so at night? My tenants are all complaining; something will have to be done."

"People are most unreasonable."

She was as furious as a cow whose calf has been ill-treated.

"Who is it that suffers most, I'd like to know? Myself and my husband! It is most ill-natured of tenants to complain."

Standing the baby on her knee and kissing her violently, "Oose never been werry seepsy at night has Oo, Puss Ducksey?"

The child smacked the mother's face with extraordinary vigour, leaving a red streak across the cheek. The mother kissed the cruel little fist.

"Something will have to be done, otherwise I shall have an empty house," I repeated determinedly for the third time.

"What, for instance?"

"A few spankings."

The woman's face boiled red.

"Spank Puss! Never!"

My hand itched to spank both child and mother.

"Why don't you train the child? It is not fair to her, only makes people dislike her."

"As if any one could dislike Puss, our darling!" She looked hate at me.

During our conversation Puss had been staring at me with all her pale eyes, her brow wrinkled. Now she scrambled from her mother's lap to the floor and by some strange, crablike movement contrived not only to reach me but to drag herself up by my skirt and stand at my knee staring up into my face.

"Look! Look! Puss has taken her first steps alone and to you, you, who hate her," said the angry mother.

"I don't hate the youngster. Only I cannot have a spoiled child rob me of my livelihood and you must either train her or go elsewhere."

She clutched the honey-haired creature to her.

"The people upstairs have left because of your baby's

crying at night. They gave no notice. How could I expect it: the man has to go to business whether your child has yelled all night or not. Another tenant is going too. I wish I could leave myself!"

I saw that my notice was being ignored. I had sent it in when I served her last rent. Go she must! It was in her hand when she came up to pay.

"Of course you don't mean this?" She held out the notice.

"I do."

"But have you not observed an improvement? She only cried four times last night."

"Yes, but each time it lasted for a quarter of the night."

"Sweet Pussy!" she said, and smothered the scowling face with kisses. "They don't want us, Puss!"

"That notice stands," I said, looking away from Puss. "I got no notices from the tenants Puss drove away."

The angry mother rushed for the door. I went to open it for her and a little pink finger reached across her mother's shoulder and gave me a little, pink poke and a friendly gurgling chuckle.

"What I cannot understand," the woman blazed at me as she turned the corner, "is *why* Puss, my shy baby who won't allow any one to speak to her, appears actually to *like* you, you who hate her."

But did I hate the little girl with honey-coloured hair? She had cost me two tenants and no end of sleep, had heated my temper to boiling, yet, somehow I could not hate that baby. The meanest thing about her was the way she could make you feel yourself. One has to make a living and one must sleep. It is one of the crookednesses of life when a little yellow-haired baby can cause you so much trouble and yet won't even let you hate her.

Puss sailed off to her new home in a pram propelled by an angry parent.

"Ta ta," she waved as they turned the corner—and I? I kissed my hand to Puss when her mother was not looking.

Bachelors

WHEN A flat housed a solitary bachelor, there was a curious desolation about it. The bachelor's front door banged in the morning and again at night. All day long there was deadly stillness in that flat, that secret silence of "Occupied" emptiness, quite a different silence from "To Let" emptiness.

Pedlars passed the flat without calling. The blinds dipped or were hoisted at irregular levels. Sometimes they remained down all day. Sometimes they were up all night. There were no callers and there was no garbage. Men ate out.

Bachelors that rent flats or houses do so because they are home-loving; otherwise they would live in a boarding-house and be "done" for. They are tired of being tidied by landladies; they like to hang coats over chair backs and find them there when they come home. It is much handier to toss soiled shirts behind the dresser than to stuff them into a laundry bag; men do love to prowl round a kitchen. A gas stove, even if it is all dusty over the top from unuse, is home-like, so is the sink with its taps, the saucepan, the dishes. The men do not want to cook, but it is nice to know they could do so if they wished. In the evening, when I tended the furnace, I heard the bachelor tramp, tramp, tramping from room to room as if searching for something. This would have fidgeted a wife, but, if the bachelor had had a wife he would probably not have tramped.

During the twenty-odd years that I rented apartments I housed quite a few bachelors. Generally they stayed a long while and their tenancy ended in marriage and in buying themselves a home.

A bachelor occupied Lower West for several years. Big, pink and amiable, he gave no trouble. Occasionally his sister would come from another town to visit him. He boarded her with me up in my flat. I enjoyed these visits, so did her brother. I saw then how domestic and home-loving the man was. He loved his sister and was very good to my Bobtail dogs. Once the sister hinted—there *was* "somebody," but, she did not know for certain; brother thought he was too old to marry—all fiddlesticks! She hoped he would. Therefore, I was not surprised when the bachelor came into my garden, and, ducking down among the dogs to hide how red he was, said, "I am going to be married. Am I an old fool?"

"Wise, I think."

"Thank you," he said, grinning all over—"I have been happy here."

He gave formal notice, saying, "I have bought a house."

"I hope you will be very happy."

"Thanks. I think we shall."

He went to the garden gate, turned, such a sparkle in his eye it fairly lit the garden.

"She's fine," he said. "Not too young—sensible."

Then he bolted. I heard the door of his flat slam as if it wanted to shut him away from the temptation of babbling to the world how happy he was.

The wedding was a month distant. During that month, when I tended the furnace there was no tramp, tramp, tramp overhead. I heard instead the contented scrunch, scrunch of his rocking chair.

The morning of the wedding he bounded up my stair, most tremendously shaved and brushed, stood upon my doormat bashfully hesitant. I did not give him the chance to get any pinker before I said, "You *do* look nice."

"Do I really?" He turned himself slowly for inspection.

"Hair, tie, everything O.K.?"

"Splendid." But I took the clothes brush from the hall stand and flicked it across his absolutely speckless shoulders. It made him feel more fixed.

His groomsman shouted from the bottom of the stair, "Hi there!" He hurried down and the two men got into a waiting cab.

Bangs and Snores

A YOUNG lawyer and his mother lived in Lower West. They were big, heavy-footed people. Every night between twelve and two the lawyer son came home to the flat. First he slammed the gate, then took the steps at a noisy run, opened and shut the heavy front door with such a bang that the noise reverberated through the whole still house. Every soul in it was startled from his sleep. People complained. I went to the young man's mother and asked that she beg the young man to come in quietly. She replied, "My son is my son! We pay rent! Good-day."

He kept on banging the house awake at two A.M.

One morning at three A.M. my telephone rang furiously. In alarm I jumped from my bed and ran to it. A great yawn was on the other end of the wire. When the yawn was spent, the voice of the lawyer's mother drawled, "My son informs me your housedog is snoring; kindly wake the dog, it disturbs my son."

The dog slept on the storey above in a basket, his nose snuggled in a heavy fur rug. I cannot think that the noise could have been very disturbing to anyone on the floor below.

The next morning I went down and had words with the woman regarding her selfish, noisy son as against my dog's snore.

Petty unreasonableness nagged calm more than all the hard work of the house. I wanted to loose the Bobtails, follow them—run, and run, and run into forever—beyond sound of every tenant in the world—tenants tore me to shreds.

Zig-Zag . . . Ki-Hi

SIMULTANEOUSLY, two young couples occupied, one Lower East, one Lower West. The couples were friends. One pair consisted of a selfish wife and an unselfish husband. The other suite housed a selfish husband and an unselfish wife.

Zig-zag, zig-zag. There was always pulling and pushing, selfishness against unselfishness.

I used to think, "What a pity the two selfish ones had not married, and the two unselfish." Then I saw that if this had been the case nobody would have got anywhere. The unselfish would have collided, rushing to do for each other. The selfish would have glowered from opposite ends of their flat, refusing to budge. . . .

Best as it was, otherwise there would have been pain—stagnation.

The unselfish wife was a chirping, cheerful creature. I loved to hear her call "Ki-hi, Ki-hi! Taste my jam tarts." And over the rail of my balcony would climb a handful of little pies, jam with criss-cross crust over the top! Or I would cry over the balcony rail, "Ki-hi, Ki-hi! Try a cake of my newest batch of home-made soap."

We were real neighbours, always Ki-hi-ing, little exchanges that sweetened the sour of landladying. This girl-wife had more love than the heart of her stupid husband could accommodate. The overflow she gave to me and to my Bobtails. She did want a baby so, but did not have one. The selfish wife shook with anxiety that a child might be born to her.

Zig-zag, zig-zag. Clocks do not say "tick, tick, tick," eternally—they say "tick, tock, tick, tock." We, looking at the clock's face, only learn the time. Most of us know nothing of a clock's internal mechanism, do not know why it says "tick, tock," instead of "tick, tick, tick."

Lady Loo, my favourite Bobtail mother, was heavy in whelp. Slowly the dog padded after my every footstep. I had prepared her a comfortable box in which to cradle her young. She was satisfied with the box, but restless. She wanted to be within sight of me, or where she heard the sound of my voice. It gave the dog comfort.

Always at noon on Sundays I dined with my sisters in our old home round the corner. I shut Lady Loo in her pen in the basement; I would hurry back. When I re-entered the basement, "Ki-hi!"—a head popped in the window of Loo's pen. On the pavement outside sat little "Ki-hi."

"Loo whimpered a little, was lonely when she heard you go. I brought my camp stool and book to keep her company. Ki-hi, Lady Loo! Good luck!" She was away!

I think that little kindness to my mother Bobtail touched me deeper than anything any tenant ever did for me.

Blind

MOTHER and daughter came looking for a flat, not in the ordinary way—asking about this and that, looking out of the windows to see what view they would have. They did not note the colour of the walls, but poked and felt everything, smoothed their fingers over surfaces, spaced the distance of one thing from another. I sensed they sought something particular; they kept exchanging glances and nods, asked questions regarding noises. They went away and I forgot about them. Towards evening they came back; they were on their way to the Seattle boat, had decided to take my flat, and wanted to explain something to me. The cab waited while we sat on my garden bench.

"There will be three people in the flat," said the woman. "My mother, my daughter and my daughter's fiancé."

"It is necessary to get the young man away from his present environment; he has been very, very ill."

She told me that while he was making some experiments recently something had burst in his face, blowing his eyes out. The shock had racked the young man's nerves to pieces. His fiancée was the only person who could do anything with him. She was devoted. The grandmother would keep house for them. They asked me to buy and prepare a meal so that they could come straight from the boat next day and not have to go to a restaurant.

The meal was all ready on the table when the girl led the crouching huddle that was her sweetheart into the flat. Old grandmother paddled behind—a regular emporium of curiosities. She looked like the bag stall in a bazaar; she was carrying all kinds—paper, leather, string and cloth. They dangled from her hands by cords and loops, or she could never have managed them all. She hung one bag or two over each door-knob as she passed through the flat, and then began taking off various articles of her clothing. As she took each garment off, she cackled, "Dear me, now I must remember where I put that!" Her hat was on the drainboard, her shoes on the gas stove, her cloak on the writing desk, her dress hung over the top of the cooler door. Her gloves and purse were on the dinner-table, and her spectacles sat on top of the loaf. She looked pathetic, plucked. After complete unbuilding came reconstruction. She attacked the bags, pulling out a dressing sacque, a scarf, an apron and something she put on her head. She seemed conscious of her upper half only, perhaps she used only a handmirror. Her leg half was pathetic and ignored. The scant petticoat came only to her knees, there was a little fence of crocheted lace around each knee. Black stockings hung in lengthwise folds around the splinters of legs that were stuck into her body and broke at right angles to make feet. Her face-skin was yellow and crinkled as the shell of an almond—the chin as pointed as an almond's tip.

The girl led the boy from room to room. She held one of his hands, with the other he was feeling, feeling everything that he could reach. So were his feet—shuffling over the carpet, over the polished floor. Grannie and I kept up a conversation, turning from him when we spoke so that he could hear our voices coming from behind our heads and not feel as if we were watching him.

Grannie "clucked" them in to dinner; I came away.

It was natural enough that the blind man should be fussy over sounds. Grannie flew up to my flat and down like a whiz cash-box. The wind caught her as she turned the corner of my stairs, exposing a pink flannelette Grannie one week and a blue flannelette Grannie the next. She was very spry, never having to pause for breath before saying,

"Tell those folks above us to wear slippers—tell them to let go their taps gently—have a carpenter fix that squeaky floor board."

Then she whizzed downstairs and the door gave back that jerky smack that says, "Back again with change!"

On Sunday morning the house was usually quiet. Settling in families was always more or less trying. I determined to have a long late lie, Grannie and family being well established. At seven A.M. my bell pealed violently. I stuck my head out into the drizzling rain and called, "What is wanted?"

Grannie's voice squeaked—"You!"

"Anything special? I am not up."

"Right away! Important!"

I hurried. Anything might have happened with that boy in the state he was.

When I opened the door, Grannie poked an empty vase at me, "The flowers you put in our flat are dead. More!"

The girl and the boy sat in my garden at the back of the house. It was quiet and sheltered there, away from the stares the boy could not bear. The monkey was perched in her cherry-tree, coy as Eve, gibbering if some one pulled in the clothes-line which made her tree shiver and the cherries bob, stretching out her little hands for one of the pegs she had coveted all the while that the pyjamas, the dresses and aprons had been drying. The girl told him about it all, trying to lighten his awful dark by making word-pictures for him—the cat on the fence, the garden, flowers, me weeding, the monkey in her cherry-tree.

"Is that monkey staring at me?"

"No, she is searching the dry grass round the base of the cherry-tree for earwigs now. Hear her crunch that one! Now she is peeping through the lilac bush, intensely interested in something. Oh, it's the Bobtails!"

I had opened the gates from dog-field and puppy-pen. Bobtails streamed into the garden. People sitting with idle hands suggested fondling, which dogs love. They ringed themselves around the boy and girl. The mother dog led her pups up to them—the pups tugged at his shoelaces, the mother dog licked his hand. He was glad to have them come of themselves. He could stoop and pick them up without someone having to put them into his arms. He buried his blackness in the soft black of their live fur. A pup licked his face, its sharp new teeth pricked his fingers, he felt its soft clinging tongue, smelled the puppy breath. The old dog sat with her head resting on his knee. He could feel her eyes on him; he did not mind those eyes. The sun streamed over everything. His taut nerves relaxed. He threw back his head and laughed!

The girl gathered a red rose, dawdled it across his cheek and forehead. She did not have to tell him the colour of the rose; it had that exultant rich red smell. He put his nose among the petals and drew great breaths.

Suddenly the back door of their flat flew open— PLOSH!—Out among the flowers flew Grannie's dish-water. Grannie was raised in drought. She could not bear to waste water down a drain.

Old Grannie over-fussed the young folks. She was kind, but she had some trying ways. Afternoon house-cleaning was one of them.

The new bride in Lower East was having her post-nuptial "at home" and Grannie must decide that very afternoon to house-clean her front room. She heaved the rugs and chairs out onto the front lawn; all the bric-a-brac followed. She tied the curtains in knots and, a cloth about her head, poised herself on a table right in front of the window. Everyone could see the crochet edging dangling over the flutes of black stocking. She hung out—she took in; her arms worked like pistons. The bride's first guest met a cloud of Bon Ami as Gran shook her duster. The waves from Gran's scrub bucket lapped to the very feet of the next guest—dirty waves that had already washed the steps. The bride came up the next day to see me about it.

Why—oh, why—oh, why—could one not secure tenants in packets of "named varieties"—true to type like asters and sweet peas? The House of All Sorts got nothing but "mixed."

Snow

TALL—LOOSEKNIT—dark-skinned—big brown eyes that could cry grandly without making her face ugly—sad eyes that it took nothing at all to fire and make sparkle.

That funny joker, life, had mated her to a scrunched-up whipper-snapper of a man, with feet that took girls' boots and with narrow, white hands. They had a fiery-haired boy of six. His mother spoiled him. It was so easy for her to fold her loose-knit figure down to his stature. They had great fun. The father scorned stooping. Neither his body nor his mind was bendable.

I heard mother and son joking and sweeping snow from their steps. Sweeping, snowballing—sweeping, laughing. That was on Monday. By Wednesday more snow had fallen, and she was out again sweeping furiously—but she was alone.

"Where is your helper?"

"Sick."

"Anything serious?"

"I have sent for the doctor. I am clearing the snow so that he can get in." She had finished now and went in to her flat and banged the door angrily—evident anger, but not at me.

The doctor came and went; I ran down to her.

"What does the doctor say?"

"Nothing to be alarmed over."

She was out in the snow again. Little red-head was at the window; both were laughing as if they shared some very good joke. Then I saw what she was doing. She was filling snow back into the path she had cleared in the morning, piling the snow deeper than it was before, spanking it down with the shovel to keep it from blowing away. She carried snow from across the lawn, careful not to leave any clear path to her door.

"Why are you doing that?"

Her eyes sparkled; she gave the happiest giggle and a nod to her boy.

"My husband would not get up and shovel a path for the doctor. Do you think he is going to find a clear path when he comes home to lunch? Not if I know it, he isn't."

"If it were not already finished, I would be delighted to help," I said and we both ran chuckling into our own flats.

Arabella Jones's Home

ARABELLA JONES ran out of the back door, around the house and into the front door of her flat. Over and over she did it. Each time she rang her own door bell and opened her own front door and walked in with a laugh as if such a delightful thing had never happened to her before.

"It is half like having a house of my own," she said, and rushed into the garden to gather nasturtiums. She put them into a bowl and dug her nose down among the blossoms. "Bought flowers don't smell like that, and oh, oh, the kitchen range! and a pulley clothes-line across the garden! my own bath! Nothing shared—no gas plate hidden behind a curtain—no public entrance and no public hall! Oh, it is only the beginning too; presently we shall own a whole house and furniture and our own garden, not rented but our very own!"

It was not Silas Jones but "a home" that had lured Arabella into marriage. When dull, middle-aged Silas said, "I am tired of knocking round, I want a home and a wife inside that home—what about it, Arabella?" she lifted her face to his like a "kiss-for-a-candy" little girl. And they were married.

That was in Eastern Canada—they began to move West. It was fun living in hotels for a bit, but soon Arabella asked, "When are we going to get the home?"

"We have to find out first where we want it to be."

The place did not matter to Arabella. She wanted a home. They travelled right across Canada, on, on, till they came to Vancouver and the end of the rail.

"Now there is no further to go, can we get our home?"

"There is still Vancouver Island," he said.

They took the boat to Victoria. Here they were in "Lower West," while Silas Jones looked around. He was in no hurry to buy. The independence of a self-contained flat would satisfy his young wife for the time being.

Arabella Jones kept begging me, "Do come down to our flat of an evening and talk before my husband about the happiness of owning your own home."

Mortgage, taxes, tenants, did not make home-owning look too nice to me just then—I found it difficult to enthuse.

Silas had travelled. He was a good talker, but I began to notice a queerness about him, a "far-offness"—when his eyes glazed, his jaw dropped and he forgot. Arabella said, "Silas is sleeping badly, has to take stuff." She said too, "He is always going to Chinatown," and showed me vases and curios he bought in Chinatown for her.

One night Silas told me he had been looking round, and expected to buy soon, so I could consider my flat free for the first of the next month should I have an applicant.

The following day I was going down my garden when he called to me from his woodshed. I looked up—drew back. His face was livid—eyes wild; foam came from his lips.

"Hi, there, you!" he shouted. "Don't you dare come into my flat, or I'll kill you—kill you, do you hear? None of your showing off of my flat!"

He was waving an axe round his head, looking murderous. I hurried past, did not speak to him. I went to the flat at the other side of the house; this tenant knew the Joneses.

I said, "Silas Jones has gone crazy or he is drunk."

"You know what is the matter with that man, don't you?"

"No, what?"

"He"—a tap at the door stopped her. Silas Jones's young wife was there.

"Somebody wants to see over our flat," she said.

"Would you be kind enough to show it to them?"

"It would be better for you to do it yourself," she said shortly. I saw she was angry about something.

"I can't—your husband—"

"My husband says you insulted him—turned your back on him when he spoke to you. He is very angry."

"I do not care to talk to drunken men."

"Drunken? My—husband—does—not—drink. . . ." She spoke slowly as if there were a wonder between every word; her eyes had opened wide and her face gone white. "I will show the flat," she said.

I stood on the porch waiting while the women went over the Joneses' flat. Suddenly, Silas was there—gripping my shoulder, his terrible lips close to my ear.

"You told. . . !"

His wife was coming—he let go of me. I went back to my other tenant.

"What was it you were going to tell me about Silas Jones?"

"Dope."

"Dope! I have never seen any one who took dope."

"You have now—you have let the cat out of the bag, too. Did you see the girl's face when you accused her husband of being drunk? She was putting two and two together—his medicine for insomnia—his violent tempers —Chinatown. . . . Poor child. . . ."

I kept well out of the man's way. He was busy with agents. His wife was alternately excited about the home and very sad.

I knew it was her step racing up the stairs. "My husband has bought a house, furniture and all. It is a beauty. It has a garden. Now I shall have a home of my very own!"

She started to caper about . . . stopped short . . . her hands fell to her sides, her face went dead. She stood before the window looking, not seeing.

"I came to ask if you know of a woman I could get, one who would live in. My husband wants to get a Chinaman to do the work, but I . . . I *must* have a woman."

Her lips trembled, great fear was in her eyes.

She came back to see me a few days after they had moved, full of the loveliness of the new home.

"You must come and see it—you will come, won't you?"

"I had better not."

"Because of Silas?"

"Yes."

"If I 'phone some day when he is going to be out, please, will you come?"

"Yes."

She never telephoned. They had been in their new home less than a month when this notice caught my eyes in the newspaper:

"For sale by public auction, house, furniture and lot."

The name of the street and the number of the house were those of Arabella Jones's new home.

Awful Partic'lar

"PRICE of flat?"

"Twenty-five a month."

"Take twenty?"

"No."

"Twenty-two?"

"No."

"Quiet house? No children? No musical instruments? No mice? My folks is partic'lar, awful partic'lar—awful *clean!* . . . They's out huntin' too—maybe they's found somethin' at twenty. Consider twenty-three?"

"No. Twenty-five is my price, take it or leave it."

He went back to pinch the mattress again, threw himself into an easy chair and moulded his back into the cushions. . . . "Comfortable chair! Well, guess I better go and see what's doin' with the folks. Twenty-three-fifty? Great to get partic'lar tenants, you know."

I waved him to the door.

Soon he was back with his wife, dry and brittle as melba toast, and a daughter, dull and sagging. Both women flopped into easy chairs and lay back, putting their feet up on another chair; they began to press their shoulder-blades into the upholstery, hunting lumps or loose springs. Meanwhile their noses wriggled like rabbits, inflated nostrils spread to catch possible smells, eyes rolling from object to object critically. After resting, they went from one thing to another, tapping, punching; blankets got smelled, rugs turned over, cupboards inspected, bureau drawers and mirrors tested.

"Any one ever die in this apartment?"

"No."

"Any one ever sick here?" The woman spat her questions.

"Any caterwauling at nights?"

"We do not keep cats."

"Then you have mice—bound to."

"Please go. I don't want you for tenants!"

"Hoity, toity! Give my folks time to look around. They's partic'lar. I telled you so."

The woman and the girl were in the kitchen insulting my pots and pans. The woman stuck a long thin nose into the garbage pail. The girl opened the cupboards.

"Ants? Cockroaches?"

I flung the outer door wide. "Go! I won't have you as tenants!"

Melba toast scrunched. Pa roared. "You can't do that! You can't do that! The card says 'Vacant.' We've took it."

His hand went reluctantly into his pocket, pulled out a roll of bills, laid two tens upon the table; impertinently leering an enquiring "O.K.?", he held out his hand for the key. I stuck it back into my pocket—did not deign an answer. Slowly he fumbled with the bill-roll, laid five ones on the table beside the two tens. Between each laying down he paused and looked at me. When my full price was on the table I put my hand in my pocket, handed him the key.

At six o'clock the next morning the "partic'lar woman" jangled my doorbell as if the house was on fire.

"There's a rust spot on the bottom of the kettle—Old Dutch."

I gave her a can of Old Dutch. She was scarcely gone before she was back.

"Scoured a hole clean through. Give me another kettle."

Hardly was she inside her door before the old man came running. "She says which is hot and which cold?"

"Tell her to find out!"

No other tenant in that or any other flat in my house left the place in such filth and disorder as those *partic'lar* people.

Gran's Battle

THE FAMILY in Lower West consisted of a man, a woman and a child. A week after they moved in, the woman's sister came to stay with her. She was straight from hospital and brought a new-born infant with her—a puny, frail thing, that the doctor shook his head over.

Immediately the baby's grandma was sent for, being, they declared, the only person who could possibly pull the baby through. Grandma could not leave her young son and a little adopted girl, so she brought them along.

The flat having but one bedroom, a kitchen and living-room, the adults slept by shifts. The children slept on sofas, or on the floor, or in a bureau drawer. Gran neither sat nor lay—she never even thought of sleep; she was there to save the baby. The man of the family developed intense devotion to his office, and spent most of his time there after Gran moved in.

We were having one of our bitterest cold snaps. Wind due north, shrieking over stiff land; two feet of snow, all substances glibbed with ice and granite-hard. I, as land-lady, had just two jobs—shovelling snow—shovelling coal. Gran's job was shooing off death—blowing up the spark of life flickering in the baby.

No one seemed to think the baby was alive enough to hear sounds. Maybe Gran thought noise would help to scare death. The cramming of eight souls into a three-room flat produced more than noise—it was bedlam!

The baby was swaddled in cotton-wool saturated with the very loudest-smelling brand of cod-liver oil. The odour of oil permeated the entire house. The child was tucked into his mother's darning-basket which was placed on the dining table.

The infant's cry was too small to be heard beyond the edge of the table. We in the rest of the house might have thought him dead had not Gran kept us informed of her wrestling, by trundling the heavy table up and down the polished floor day and night. The castor on each of the table-legs had a different screech, all four together a terrible quartette with the slap, slap of Gran's carpet slippers marking time. Possibly Gran thought perpetual motion would help to elude death's grip on the oiled child.

Periodically the aunt of the infant came upstairs to my flat to telephone the doctor. She sat hunched on the stool in front of the 'phone, tears rolled out of her eyes, sploshed upon her chest.

"Doctor, the baby is dying—his mother cries all the time—when he dies she will die too. . . . Oh, yes, Gran is here, she never leaves him for a minute; night and day she watches and wheels him on the table."

The whole house was holding its breath, waiting on the scrap of humanity in the darning basket. Let anybody doze off, Grandma was sure to drop a milk bottle, scrunch a tap, tread on a child! The house had to be kept tropical. Gran was neither clothed nor entirely bare. She took off and took off, her garments hung on the backs of all the chairs. She peeled to the limit of the law, and snatched food standing. Three whole weeks she waged this savage one-man battle to defeat death—she won—the infant's family were uproarious with joy.

Gran toppled into bed for a long, long sleep. Mother and aunt sat beside the darning basket planning the baby's life from birth to death at a tremendous age.

Gran woke refreshed—vigorous, clashed the pots and pans, banged doors, trundled the table harder than ever, and sang lullabies in a thin high voice, which stabbed our ears like neuralgia.

The House of All Sorts was glad the child was to live. They had seen the crisis through without a murmur. Now, however, they came in rebellion and demanded peace. The doctor had said the child could go home with safety—my tenants said he must go! I marched past twelve dirty milk-bottles on the ledges of the front windows. Gran opened, and led me to the basket to see the infant, red now instead of grey.

I said, "Fine, fine! All the tenants are very glad, and now, when is he going home?"

"Doctor says he could any day. We have decided to keep him here another month."

"No! A three-room flat cannot with decency house eight souls. I rented my flat to a family of three. This noise and congestion must cease."

Grandmother, mother, aunt all screeched reproaches. I was a monster, turning a new-born infant out in the snow. They'd have the law.

"The snow is gone. His mother has a home. His grandmother has a home. I rented to a family of three. The other tenants have been kindly and patient. The child has had his chance. Now we want quiet."

My tenant, the aunt of the baby, said, "I shall go too!"

"Quite agreeable to me."

A "vacancy" card took the place of the twelve dirty milk bottles in the front window of Lower East.

Peach Scanties

COMING up Simcoe Street I stopped short and nearly strangled! There, stretched right across the front windows of the Doll's Flat, the street side of my respectable apartment house, dangled from the very rods where my fresh curtains had been when I went out—one huge suit of men's natural wool underwear, one pair of men's socks, one pair of women's emaciated silk stockings, a vest, and two pairs of peach scanties.

Who, I wondered, had gone up the street during the two hours of my absence? Who had seen my house shamed?

I could not get up the stairs fast enough, galloping all the way! There was only enough breath left for: "Please, *please* take them down."

I pointed to the wash.

Of course she was transient—here today, gone tomorrow —not caring a whoop about the looks of the place.

"I like our underwear sunned," she said with hauteur.

"There are lines out in the back."

"I do not care for our clothes to mix with everybody's —and there are the stairs."

"I will gladly take them down and hang them for you."

"Thanks, I prefer them where they are. It is *our* flat. We have the right—"

"But the appearance! The other tenants!"

"My wash is clean. It is darned. Let them mind their own business, and you yours."

"It *is* my business—this house is my livelihood."

The woman shrugged.

Merciful night came down and hid the scanties and the rest.

Next wash-day the same thing happened. The heavy woolies dripped and trickled over the tenant's clean washed windows below; of course she rushed up—furious as was I!

Again I went to the Doll's Flat. I refused to go away until the washing was taken down and the curtains hung up. "If you live in this house you must comply with the ways of it," I said.

On the third week she hung her wash in the windows the same as before. I gave her written notice.

"I shall not go."

"You will, unless you take that wash down and never hang it on my curtain rods again!"

Sullenly, she dragged the big woollen combination off the rod, threw it on the table; its arms and legs kicked and waved over the table's edge, then dangled dead. Down came the lank stockings, the undervest—last of all the peach scanties. Both pairs were fastened up by the same peg. She snapped it off viciously. A puff of wind from the open door caught and ballooned the scanties; off they sailed, out the window billowing into freedom. As they passed the hawthorn tree its spikes caught them. There they hung over my front gate, flapping, flapping—"Oh dear! Oh dear! Oh dear!"

Sham

AS THE world war progressed rentals went down till it became impossible to meet living expenses without throwing in my every resource. I had no time to paint so had to rent the studio flat and make do myself with a basement room and a tent in my back garden. Everything together only brought in what a flat and a half had before the war.

A woman came to look at the Studio flat and expressed herself delighted with it.

"Leave your pretty things, won't you?" she begged with a half sob. "I have nothing pretty now and am a widow, a Belgian refugee with a son in the army."

She spoke broken English. We were all feeling very tender towards the Belgians just then.

"Come and see me; I am very lonely," she said and settled into the big studio I had built for myself. I granted her request for a substantial cut off the rental because of her widowhood, her country and her soldier son. Poor, lisping-broken-English stranger! I asked her several questions about Belgium. She evaded them. When she did not remember she talked perfect English, but when she stopped to think, the words were all mixed and broken. When she met any one new her sputterings were almost incoherent. I asked her, "How long since you left Belgium?" She hesitated, afraid of giving away her age, which I took to be fifty-five or thereabouts.

"I was born in Belgium of English parents. We left Belgium when I was four years old."

"You have never been back since?"

"No."

She saw me thinking.

"How the first language one hears sticks to the tongue!" she remarked. "It's queer, isn't it?"

"Very!"

As far as I was concerned, I let her remain the brave little Belgian widow with a son fighting on our side, but the son came back to his mother, returned without thanks from training camp, a schoolboy who had lied about his age and broken down under training. Now the widow added to her pose, "Belgian refugee widow with a war-broken son."

Tonics and nourishing dishes to build Herb up were now her chief topic of conversation with her tenant neighbours. Daily, at a quarter to twelve, one or the other of us could expect a tap on our door and . . . would we lend the mother of Herb a cup of rice, or macaroni, or tapioca, an egg for his "nog" or half a loaf. The baker was always missing her, or the milkman forgot. We got sick of her borrowings and bobbed below the windows when she passed up the stair, but she was a patient knocker and kept on till something on the gas stove began to burn and the hider was obliged to come from hiding. She never dreamed of returning her borrowings. The husbands declared they had had enough. They were not going to support her. She appeared very comfortably off, took in all the shows, dressed well, though too youthfully. Having no husband to protest I became the victim of all her borrowings, and the inroad on my rice and tapioca and macaroni became so heavy my pantry gave up keeping them.

When the "flu" epidemic came along, Herb sneezed twice. His mother knew he had it, shut him in his bedroom, poking cups of gruel in at the door and going quickly away. She told every one Herb had "flu" and she knew she was getting it from nursing him, but Herb had not got "flu" and, after a day or two, was out again. Then the widow told every one she had contracted "flu" from Herb. She hauled the bed from her room out into the middle of the Studio before the open fire and lay there in state, done up in fancy bed-jackets, smoking innumerable cigarettes and entertaining anybody whom she could persuade to visit. For six weeks she lay there for she said it was dangerous to get out of bed for six weeks if you had had "flu." The wretched Herbert came to me wailing for help.

"Get mother up," he pleaded. "Make her take her bed out of the studio; make her open the windows."

"How can I, Herbert? She has rented the flat."

"Do something," he besought. "Burn the house down— only get mother out of bed."

But she stayed her full six weeks in bed. When she saw that people recognized her sham and did not visit her any more she got up—well.

It was a year of weddings. The widow took a tremendous interest in them, sending Herb to borrow one or another of my tenants' newspapers before they were up in the morning to find out who was marrying. She attended all the church weddings, squeezing in as a guest.

"You never know who it will be next," she giggled, sparkling her eyes coyly, and running from flat to flat telling the details of the weddings.

One day she hung her head and said, "Guess." Several of us happened to be together.

"Guess what?"

"Who the next bride is to be?"

"You!" joked an old lady.

The widow drooped her head and simpered, "How *did* you guess?"

He was a friend of Herbert's and "coming home very soon," so she told us.

The house got a second shock when from somewhere the widow produced the most terrible old woman whom she introduced as "My mother, Mrs. Dingham—come to stay with me till after the wedding."

Mrs. Dingham went around the house in the most disgusting, ragged and dirty garments. Her upper part was clothed in a black sateen dressing sacque with which she wore a purple quilted petticoat. Her false teeth and hair "additions" lay upon the studio table except in the afternoons when she went out to assist the widow to buy her trousseau. Then she was elegant. Herb's expression was exasperated when he looked across the table and saw the teeth, the tin crimpers that caught her scant hair to her pink scalp. The House of All Sorts was shamed at having such a repulsive old witch scuttling up and down the stairs and her hooked nose poking over the verandah rail whenever there was a footstep on the stair. It was a relief when she put all her "additions" on and went off to shop.

I wanted my Studio back; I was homesick for it, besides I knew if I did not rescue it soon it would be beyond cleaning. Two years of the widow's occupancy had about ruined everything in it. When I heard that Herb and the old mother were to keep house there during the honeymoon, while the bridegroom was taking some six weeks' course in Seattle, I made up my mind.

The groom came—he was only a year or two older than Herb. The boys had been chums at school. He was good-looking with a gentle, sad, sad face, like a creature trapped. She delighted to show him off and you could see that when she did so they bit him to the bone, those steel teeth that had caught him. On one point he was firm, if there was to be a wedding at all it was to be a very quiet one. In everything Herb was with his friend, not his mother.

They were married. After the ceremony the old woman and daughter rushed upstairs to the studio. Herb and the groom came slowly after. The bride's silly young fixings fluttered back over their heads, and the old woman's cackle filled the garden as they swept up the stair. They had a feast in the studio to which I was not invited. I had raised the rent and they were going—violently indignant with me.

Mrs. Pillcrest's Poems

SOMETIMES a word or two in Pillcrest's poems jingled. More occasionally a couple of words made sense. They flowed from her lips in a sing-song gurgle, spinning like pennies, and slapping down dead.

Mrs. Pillcrest was a small, spare woman with opaque blue eyes. While the poems were tinkling out of one corner of her mouth a cigarette was burning in the other. The poems were about the stars, maternity, love, living, and the innocence of childhood. (Her daughter of ten and her son aged seven cursed like troopers. The first time I saw the children they were busy giving each other black eyes at my front gate while their mother was making arrangements about the flat and poeming for me.)

I said, "I do not take children."

"Canadian children . . . I can *quite* understand . . . *my* children are *English!*"

"I prefer them Canadian."

"Really!" Her eye-brows took a scoot right up under her hat. She said, "Pardon," lit a new cigarette from the stump of the last, sank into the nearest chair and burst into jingles!

I do not know why I accepted the Pillcrests, but there I was, putting in extra cots for the children—settling them in before I knew it.

The girl was impossible. They sent her away to friends.

On taking possession of the flat, Mrs. Pillcrest went immediately to bed leaving the boy of seven to do the cooking, washing, and housework. The complete depletion of hot water and perpetual smell of burning sent me down to investigate.

Mrs. Pillcrest lay in a daze of poetry and tobacco smoke. The sheets (mine) were punctured lavishly with little brown-edged holes. It seemed necessary for her to gesticulate with lighted cigarette as she "poemed."

She said, "It is lovely of you to come," and immediately made a poem about it. In the middle there was a loud stumping up the steps, and I saw Mr. Pillcrest for the first time.

He was a soldier. Twice a week the Canadian army went to pot while Dombey Pillcrest came home to visit his family. He was an ugly, beefy creature dressed in ill-fitting khaki, his neck stuck up like a hydrant out of a brown boulevard.

Poems would not "make" on Mr. Pillcrest, so Mrs. Pillcrest made them out of other things and basted him with them. He slumped into the biggest chair in the flat, and allowed the gravy of trickling poems to soothe his training-camp and domestic friction—as stroking soothes a cat.

Mrs. Pillcrest told me about their love-making. She said, "My people owned one of those magnificent English estates —hunting—green-houses—crested plate—Spode—everything! I came to visit cousins in Canada, have a gay time, bringing along trunks of ball dresses and pretty things. I met Dombey Pillcrest. . . ."

She took the cigarette from her lips, threw it away. Her hands always trembled—her voice had a pebbly rattle like sea running out over a stony beach.

"Dombey told me about his prairie farm; the poetry of its endless rolling appealed, sunsets, waving wheat! We were married. Some of the family plate, the Spode and linen came out from home for my house.

"We went to Dombey's farm . . . I did not know it would be like that . . . too big . . . poems would not come . . . space drowned everything!

"The man who did the outside, the woman who did the inside work kept the place going for a while . . . babies came . . . I began to write poems again—our help left—I had my babies and Dombey!"

She poemed to the babies. All her poems were no more than baby talk—now she had an audience. . . . The blue-eyed creatures lying in their cradle watched her lips, and cooed back.

As the children grew older they got bored by Mother's poems and by hunger. They ran away when she poemed. It hurt her that the children would not listen.

She had another bitter disappointment on that farm. "I did so want to 'lift' the Harvesters! When they came to thresh was my chance. I was determined they should have something different, something refined. For *once* they should see the *real thing,* eat off Limoges, use crested plate! I put flowers on the table, fine linen; I wrote a little poem for each place. The great brown, hungry men burst into the room—staggered back—most touching! . . . none of the bestial gorging you see among the lower classes. They stared; they ate little. Not one of them looked at a poem. If you believe it, they asked the gang foreman to request 'food, not frills' next day. Ruffians! Canadians, my dear!"

"I am Canadian," I said.

"My *deear!* I supposed you were English!"

"One day Dombey said, 'Our money is finished. We cannot hire help; we must leave the farm. You cannot work, darling!' "

They scraped up the broken implements and lean cows and had a sale. Mrs. Pillcrest sat on a broken harrow in the field and made a poem during the sale. Mr. Pillcrest wandered about, dazed. The undernourished, over-accented children got in everybody's way. When it was over, the Pillcrests came out west and hunted round to find the most English-accented spot so that their children should not be contaminated by Canada. That was Duncan, B.C., of course. War came; Dombey joined up. Here they were in my flat.

"I had *so* hoped that you were English, my dear!"

"Well, I'm *not*." Mrs. Pillcrest moaned at my tone.

Potato-paring seemed to be specially inspiring for Mrs. Pillcrest. She liked to do it at the back door of her flat, looking across my garden, poeming as she pared. She always wore a purple chiffon scarf about her throat; it had long floating tails that wound round the knife and got stabbed into holes. The thick parings went slap, slap on the boards of the verandah. The peeled flesh of the potatoes was purpled by the scarf while poems rolled out over my garden.

"Have you ever published your poems, Mrs. Pillcrest?"

"I do not write my poems. They spring direct from some hidden source, never yet located, a joyous—joyous source!"

"Curse you, Mother! Come get dinner, instead of blabbing that stuff!"

"Son—my beloved son!" Mrs. Pillcrest said, and kissed the boy's scowling face.

The Pillcrests were not with me very long because Mr. Pillcrest's training camp was moved.

Just as their time was up—the flat already re-let—Mrs. Pillcrest and son disappeared. Time went on, the new tenant was fussing for possession. After five days elapsed without sign or sound, I climbed a ladder and looked through the windows. Everything was in the greatest confusion.

I rang the barracks. "Mr. Pillcrest? Mrs. Pillcrest's tenancy expired five days ago."

"Yes? Oh, ah—Mrs. Pillcrest is visiting; she will doubtless be returning soon."

"But the flat—the new tenant is waiting . . ." I found myself talking over a dead wire.

She tripped home sparkling with poems.

"Your rent was up five days ago, Mrs. Pillcrest."

"Really! Well, well! Shall I pay five days extra?" (With some rhyme about "honey," "money" and "funny.") My patience was done—"Nothing funny about it! It is not business!"

Taut with fury Mrs. Pillcrest's poem strangled. "Business! Kindly remember, Landlady, Mr. Pillcrest and I do *not belong to that class.*"

"That is evident, but at six tonight I have promised the key to the waiting tenant! *That* is business."

Unmarried

PERHAPS the most awkward situation for the inexperienced young landlady was how to deal with "unweds." Every apartment house gets them. They are often undiscernible, even to the experienced. One learns in time to catch on to little indications. . . .

The supposed husband makes all arrangements, the supposed wife approving of everything. A woman who does not nose into the domestic arrangements of the place she is going to occupy gives the first hint, for a woman indifferent to the heating, furnishing, plumbing, cooking utensils of her home is not wifely.

My first experience of this sort was with a very prepossessing couple. Their tenancy was secured by an excessively moral old lady living in Lower West. I was out when the couple came seeking. The old lady next door showed them over. She was delighted at having made so good a "let" for me. Within a week it was put to me by the renters of the other suites, "Them or us?" The couple left.

My second experience of the same kind posed as brother and widowed sister, just out from the Old Country. They offered Old Country references which would have taken six weeks to verify, yet they wanted immediate possession. Things looked all right—I was unsuspicious. You can't ask to see people's marriage certificates. They had my studio flat. It had the required number of rooms and they were delighted with the studio. I had removed myself to a tent in the garden and a gas-ring in the basement for the summer months, ends being difficult to make meet.

The couple had not been in a week before Mrs. "Below" and Mrs. "Next Door" rushed simultaneously to the garden to "tell" and bumped nose to nose.

The House of All Sorts was in ferment. If I was going to cater to that class—!

I went to the hotel the couple had stayed at before taking my flat. Here they had registered as man and wife. I took my perplexity to an experienced apartment-house landlady.

"Mm. . . . We all get them."

"How are they got rid of? Must I wait until their month is up to serve the customary notice?"

"Mm. . . ! If you can prove they are 'that kind' you need give no notice at all, but be sure—libel suits are ugly. Send your janitor into their suite on some pretext or other."

"I am my own janitor."

"Mm!"

I told her I had been to the hotel and how the couple had registered. Again the experienced one said, "Mm." I went home. I could "Mm" there just as well myself.

Mrs. Doubtful was chatty, always running down to my garden to ask advice about cookery. Brother John was fond of this or that, and how was it made? She asked me queer questions too. Was it possible to get lost in British Columbia? To take a cabin in the far woods and disappear? It would be so amusing to vanish!

Between the Doll's Flat and my studio was a locked door, a sofa backed up to the door. The Doubtfuls liked to sit on this sofa and converse. It appeared that Mrs. Doll's Flat's favourite chair was just the other side of the door. Sitting here her ear was level with the keyhole. The man said to the woman:

"Go to the garden, darling. Chat casually with our land-lady. Watch her face, her manner."

The woman returned.

"Well?"

"She suspects."

The man came to me.

"How long notice is required?"

"None."

The man bowed. No one saw them go. They left no forwarding address.

Studio

IT WOULD not be fair to the House of All Sorts were I to omit describing its chief room—the Studio—around which the house had been built. The purpose of its building had been to provide a place in which I could paint and an income for me to live on. Neither objective was ever fully realized in the House of All Sorts.

From the front of the house you got no hint that it contained the finest studio in the town. The tell-tale great north light was at the back of the house and overlooked my own garden, dominating its every corner. There were open fields surrounding my garden—fields that were the playgrounds of my Bobtail Sheep-dogs, kenneled behind the lilacs and apple-trees at the foot of the garden. It was not a very large garden, centred by a lawn which again was centred by a great olivet cherry tree. In the crotch of the tree a shelter box was fixed for the comfort of my monkey, Woo, during the summer months.

The garden was fenced and gated. It belonged exclusively to the animals and myself. No one intruded there. Visitors or tenants who came to pay or to grumble mounted the long outside stair, that met the paved walk on the west side of the house, and took their complaints to me in the studio. The garden seemed more exclusively mine than the studio. People came to the studio to see me on business; if I wanted to see myself I went to the garden. If I was angry I seized a spade and dug my anger into the soil. When I was sad the garden earth swallowed my tears, when I was merry the garden lawn danced with bouncing dogs, monkey, the Persian cat, Adolphus, and me. We did have good times in that old garden. It was in fact but a projection of my studio into the open at ground level. The square ugliness of the apartment house cut us off from the publicity of tenants and the street. High board fences determined the garden's depth and width.

The studio was a high room; its east end was alcoved and had five casement windows in a row, out of them you looked across two vacant lots to Beacon Hill Park. Every bit of the Park was stuffed with delicious memories—not its present sophistication with cultivated lawns, formal lakes, flowerbeds, peacocks and swans. Wild wind-tossed trees, Creator-planted, and very old, tangled bushes were what my memory saw. It saw also skunk cabbage swamps, where frogs croaked in chorus all the summer nights, and owls hooted. I saw too the wicked old "Park Hotel" roaring its tipsy trade. Now where it had stood the land had gone back to respectable brambles that choked everything.

The studio had to be an "everything-for-everybody" place. Its walls were cut by five doors and five windows in addition to a great north light. It was not a good room for showing pictures but fine to paint in. The walls were buff, very high and very crowded: I had no other place to store pictures than on the walls.

The centre space of the room was high emptiness. To ease congestion I suspended my extra chairs from the ceiling. There they dangled, out of the way till wanted, when they were lowered to the floor. Each worked on a pulley of its own.

In one corner of the room was an immense black-topped table, rimmed and legged with massive polished maple wood.

It was an historical table but I forget exactly why. It used to be in the Parliament Buildings and important things had been signed at it.

On top of the table was heaped every kind of article that you could think of, including Susie the white rat, whose headquarters were there. There were also huge lumps of potter's clay and unfinished potteries draped in wet rags to keep them moist during construction.

I had the great brick fire-place with the open grate blocked up. It looked very nice but used enormous quantities of fuel and heated heaven only, so I substituted an open-fronted stove which kept the studio very cosy. It was a lovable room.

In the centre of the studio floor was a long narrow black box not unlike a coffin except that it did not taper. I kept sketches in this box and on its top stood a forest of paint brushes and turpentine bottles. Between this glass-and-bristle forest and the great north light the space was particularly my own. People never walked there for fear of their shoes squeezing paint tubes or crushing charcoal. Canvases stood on two homemade bench-easels.

I never painted if any one was around and always kept my canvases carefully shrouded in dust sheets. I never did paint much in that fine studio that I had built: what with the furnace, tenants, cleaning and the garden there was no time.

The pictures on my walls reproached me. All the twenty-two years I lived in that house the Art part of me ached. It was not a bit the sort of studio I had intended to build. My architect had been as far from understanding the needs of an artist as it would be possible to believe. The people of Victoria strongly disapproved of my painting because I had gone from the old conventional way. I had experimented. Now I paused. I wished my pictures did not have to face the insulting eyes of my tenants. It made me squirm. The pictures themselves squirmed me in their own right too. They were always whispering, "Quit, quit this; come back to your own job!" But I couldn't quit; I had this house and I had no money. A living must be squeezed from somewhere.

There were two couches in my studio, one in my own special part, the other near the fireplace for visitors. The only chance I got to rest was when a visitor came. I could not leave the visitor upright while I relaxed on a sofa.

When I flung myself down, what you might have taken for a fur rug in front of the fire broke into half a dozen pieces, ran to my couch and, springing, heaped themselves on top of me—cat, dogs, monkey and rat. Life in this studio was pleasant. Its high, soft north light was good, yet it was not the sort of studio I wanted.

In Toronto I had seen the ideal artist's studio—a big room about the size of mine. There was not a picture in the room, the walls were calm restful grey. The canvases were stowed in racks in an ante-room. The furnishings were of the simplest. They consisted of a table, a large working easel, a davenport, a quiet-coloured floor covering. The building contained several studios and was set in the quiet corner of a Park. Here the artist came and shut himself in with his work; there he and his work became one. But then he did not have to run a House of All Sorts.

After twenty-two years I sold the House of All Sorts.

Art and the House

IT WAS strange that the first and only specially built, specially lighted studio I ever owned should have been a torment for me to work in. Through the studio only could you enter my four-room flat. A tap at the door—I was caught there at my easel; I felt exposed and embarrassed as if I had been discovered in my bathtub! It was a curious agony.

Possibly it was the ridicule my work had been subject to in Victoria which made me foolishly supersensitive. Even at Art School I had preferred to work in a corner, back to the wall, so that people could not look over my shoulder. In this house, if a tenant found me at my easel, I felt as though I had been cornered committing a crime.

Even while landladying, Art would keep poking me from unexpected places. Art being so much greater than ourselves, it will not give up once it has taken hold.

Victoria had been very stern about my art. Being conservative in her tastes, she hated my particular kind, she believed in having well-beaten tracks and in sticking to them.

The house was fuelling. A huge Negro came to me protesting, "Dat monk in de basement slam de winder ev'time de sacks come fo' to empty. What us do?"

I went below, moved the monkey, left Negro and monkey making friends.

By and by the man came up for me to sign his book. He stood at the studio door.

"Gee! I's envy yous."

"Because I have a monkey?"

"Because you's kin paint. Seem dat what I want all de life of me."

Later that week I was suddenly aware of two men's faces peering through my studio window. Screening hands framed their stare.

In a fury I bounced out the door on to the little balcony where the men stood.

"How dare you stare into my window? Don't you know a person's home is private? Go away."

The men fell back. Then I saw that one was my baker. The other man was a stranger.

"Pardon, Miss. We didn't mean to be rude—this 'ere feller," thumbing towards the stranger, "loves pictures. Come along, I sez, I'll show you!"

I was shamed. Humble people, here in my own town, *wanted* to see and know about Art. They might not like my special kind? What matter? They were interested in pictures.

In Victoria I had only come up against my own class. The art society, called "Island Arts and Crafts," were the exponents of Art on Vancouver Island, an extremely exclusive set. They liked what they liked—would tolerate no innovations. My change in thought and expression had angered them into fierce denouncement. To expose a thing deeper than its skin surface was to them an indecency. They ridiculed my striving for bigness, depth. The Club held exhibitions, affairs of tinkling teacups, tinkling conversation and little tinkling landscapes weakly executed in water colours. None except their own class went to these exhibitions. A baker, a coal-carrier! Good gracious! Ordinary people would never dream of straying into an "Arts and Crafts" exhibition, would have been made to feel awkward had they done so.

An idea popped into my head. I would give an exhibition for ordinary people, invite the general public, but *not* invite the Arts and Crafts. I would invite the people who walked in Beacon Hill on Saturday afternoon and on Sunday. My house was practically *in* Beacon Hill Park. Lower East had just fallen vacant. Lower West was going to be empty next week. I had a carpenter cut me a connecting door. This gave me six large, well-lighted rooms. I invited three other artists to show with me, one a portrait painter, one a lady just returned from England where she had been painting English cottage scenes, the third a flower painter. In one room I would hang my Indian canvases. Examples of my new and disliked work I would hang in the kitchens.

At the last moment the flower painter, finding that the show was not to be sponsored by the Arts and Crafts, did not show. As I read her curt, last-minute withdrawal, a young Chinese came to my door carrying a roll of paintings. He had heard about the exhibition, had come to show his work to me—beautiful water colours done in Oriental style. He was very anxious to carry his work further. He had asked admittance to the Arts and Crafts Sketching Class, and had been curtly refused because of his nationality. I invited him to show in place of the flower painter and he hung a beautiful exhibit.

The exhibition was a varied show and so successful that a few of us got together, working on the idea of starting a People's Art Gallery in these six rooms of mine. It was winter time, there were no Band Concerts in the Park. People walked until they were tired, then went home chilled. To drop in, sit by an open fire, warm, rest themselves and look at pictures, might appeal to the public. It was also suggested that there might be study classes. Young people came to see me saying how ardently they hoped the idea would be carried out.

We elected temporary officers and called a meeting of important people who could help if they would—the Lieutenant Governor, Mayor, Superintendent of Parks, a number of wealthy people with influence. We called the meeting while the exhibition was still on the walls. The rooms were thronged; there was interest; the plan was discussed. I offered Lower East and Lower West to the City at the lowest possible rental, offering also to shoulder a large proportion of the work connected with the hanging of new shows from time to time.

My friend Eric Brown, of the Canadian National Gallery at Ottawa, was enthusiastic over my plan and promised to send exhibitions out from Ottawa. But influential Victorians were uninterested, apathetic. Why, they asked, was it not sponsored by the Arts and Crafts Society? Vancouver had just built herself a fine Art Gallery. It was endowed. Unless Victoria could do something bigger and more flamboyant than Vancouver she would do nothing at all.

The Lieutenant Governor said that if the City would acquire a property and erect a fireproof building, he would be willing to lend two small etchings, very fine etchings— but he would not lend to be shown in any ordinary building.

Victoria's smart set said Beacon Hill was out of the way.

We replied, "It is handy for those who walk in the Park. You others have your cars."

The Mayor said, "The City has provided artificial lakes, a very fine pair of swans, innumerable ducks, a peacock and a Polar bear. What more could the public desire!"

The people's gallery did not materialize. The everyday public were disappointed. The wealthy closed their lips and their purses. The Arts and Crafts Society smiled a high-nosed superior smile. Lee Nam, the Chinese artist, many boys and girls and young artists were keenly disappointed.

I closed the connecting door between the suites and again rented Lower East and Lower West as dwellings.

The wise, painted eagles on my attic ceiling brooded— sorry for my disappointment. The Indians would say, "They made strong talk for me." Anyway they sent me down to the studio to forget my disappointment and to paint earnestly.

Eric Brown wrote, "I am sorry the people's gallery did not go through." He spoke kindly about my own work. I was now an invited contributor to art shows in the East. Sympathetic criticisms were unnumbing me; I desired to paint again. "After all," wrote Mr. Brown, "the people's gallery might have further crippled your own work. Victoria just is not art minded. Go ahead, paint, don't give way to discouragement. Paint, paint!"

Men Called Her Jane

NICE-LOOKING couple. He had a courtesy that was slightly foreign. She blushed readily and was gentle, had dainty smartness from shoes to the chic little hat that looked to have flown to the top of her head and perched there at just the right angle.

In my garden she bent and sniffed, "May I have a flower?"

"The madame likes flowers. You could spare her a little corner of your earth? This bit by our door, perhaps?"

"I will plant sweet peas to climb on the fence," she said happily.

Their blinds never went up till noon was well past. He claimed that work brought him home late at night—very late.

Everybody said they were an attractive-looking couple. The name he gave was "Petrie."

One day I had occasion to take "madame" some things. Her door stood open. I kept to one side while I knocked. There was no answer. I stepped forward, meaning to lay the things inside the door and go away. I saw that "madame" was in the room, arms folded across the back of a chair, head bowed, crying bitterly. I put the things down, came away.

My flat was just above the Petries'. Sometimes I thought I heard crying. Again, there would be long monotonous sounds as of someone pleading unanswered; sometimes for days everything would be deadly still.

One morning, between two and three o'clock, all the

house wrapped in sleep, shriek after shriek came from the Petries' flat. Crockery smashed. There were screams and bangs, dull murderous thuds. I jumped out of bed, ran to the room above their flat, leaned out the window.

There were three voices, two men's and a woman's. Desperate fury was in them all—low, bestial, fighting hatred.

I trembled violently, not knowing what to do. The rest of the flats were rented to women—women who expected to live here quietly, decently. It was a quiet, respectable district! How was I going to face them tomorrow, burning with shame for my house?

The door below was torn open. Bump, bump, bump! A man was ejected, thudding on each step, finally lying in a huddle on the cement walk. The door slammed. The man and the woman inside resumed their screaming and snarling.

Was he dead? I could not take my eyes off that still huddle on the pavement. By-and-by a groan—he crawled on hands and knees to the door—beat upon it with his fists.

"Jane! Jane! Listen, Jane! Let me in. Oh, Jane! Jane!" They were making such a noise they did not hear. He leant against the door, mopping his face. I could see dark stains spreading on his white handkerchief. After a long, long while he stumbled down the street.

The fighting stopped—terrible quiet—I could hear my clock ticking, or perhaps it was my heart. I went to bed hating tenants.

Next morning Petrie swaggered up to my flat, asked to use my telephone. I trembled, wondering what I was going to say to him. He 'phoned a rush order to a dry-cleaner, also for an express to take a trunk to the boat.

"You going away?" I asked.

"The madame is—we've quarrelled in fact."

"It was shameful . . . my tenants . . . ." The man shrugged.

"You wish to serve me notice?"

"Law does not require that such tenants be given notice."

The express came and took away a trunk. At dusk the woman limped down the street sagging under the weight of a heavy suitcase.

There was no sound from Lower East. All day blinds remained close drawn. The gas man came, asking that I let him into that silence to read the meter.

"The flat is still occupied, far as I know."

"Your tenant ordered his final reading this morning."

I took a pass key and went down. The place was in wild disorder. There were dozens of liquor bottles. In an attempt to be funny they had been arranged ridiculously as ornaments. Things were soiled with spilled liquor. The place smelled disgusting. The bedding was stripped from the bed. The laundry man returned it later and told me it had been soaked with blood. My carving knife belonging to the flat was missing.

Holding out a handful of carefully selected pants' buttons that he took from the meter, the gas man said, "That is what the Gas Company got. How about you, got your rent?"

"Yes, advance."

"Good," he said kindly . . . "job enough getting the liquor stains cleaned up."

I saw an envelope at my feet. In the dusk I could see the name was not Petrie, but a short name like my own. I tore it open, supposing it mine.

"Rose, my baby, my dear, why don't you write? If you did not get the job, come home, we will manage somehow. No work for Pa yet, he is sick—so am I—anxiety mostly —Rosie, come home—Mother."

I gave the letter back to the Postman.

"I opened it in the dusk by mistake; there was no forwarding address."

"I suspected," said the Postman. "Her name wasn't his name—nice-looking couple they was too . . . well . . . New to this rentin' bizness, eh? You'll larn—tough yerself to it."

His look was kind.

Furniture

ONCE I turned a zinc pail down over the head of a widow tenant.

She was on the top step of my back stair; I was on the landing above. She would neither pay nor go. The law had told me I must retain certain of her possessions until she did one thing or the other. She had given me notice; another tenant was waiting for the flat, but go the widow would not. When I did as the law directed and seized a basket full of her household goods from the back porch, she followed me upstairs screeching. It was only pots and pans, not worth the screech. "Take it then—this too," I said and popped a pail of hers, none too clean, over her head. As the pail swallowed her tatty, frizzled head she seized the basket from my arms and, blinded by the pail, sank, step by step, down, down,—bucket and widow together. She could not see where to put her feet; they pushed like flat irons into the corner of each step. It was a narrow stair. She could cling by her elbows and the basket. At the foot of the stair, a twinkle in his eyes, stood the policeman who had ordered the restraint on her goods. She raised her zinc helmet to find herself circled by his arms.

She said—"Aoow!"

Law and I laughed. Law said, "Pay, or give up the keys."

She paid and went.

A gentleman had married her. Perhaps it would be more correct to say—a gentleman married her purse full of savings. First he spent her money, then he died, leaving her with a pile of debts, a yellow-haired son and twelve rooms full of furniture.

She was angry at having a child to support, ignored the debts and adored the furniture—cheap tawdry stuff, highly varnished. She talked a great deal about "my beautiful period furniture." It was shoddy, mock, not "period," always "after," executed in imitation woods.

She moved the twelve roomfuls of furniture, piano and all, into my three-roomed Lower West Flat. Its entire floor space was packed solid to the ceiling. The yellow-haired boy crawled among the legs of furniture and bumped on bric-a-brac.

The dining-table, uncollapsible and highly varnished, the piano, the chesterfield, stuffed chairs and a few sofas made a foundation on which to heap lesser articles. On top, and on top, and on top, the heaped furniture rose to the ceiling. A narrow alleyway ran through the middle enabling her to pass through the flat—but she had to squeeze. In front of the window stood the piano. The woman could be seen and heard singing to it.

The kitchen had standing room only in front of the cook stove and at the sink. In the bedroom, she climbed over high-boys and bureaus to hurl the child into the bed beyond with a screeching of bed springs which delighted him.

She called me in to see how things were, saying "You will simply *have* to give me more storage space!"

"You have much more than your share of the basement now. You saw what space there was before you took the flat. How could you expect three rooms to accommodate the furniture of twelve? Sell what you don't need."

"Sell my furniture! My beautiful furniture! Never!"

"You don't want all of it. It only makes you uncomfortable."

"I want every bit of it—to sell would be to lose money. I shall keep every bit; I expect to entertain members of the Choral Society I belong to."

So she went on living in great discomfort. The verandah

and woodshed were crammed to bursting. The stuff was all wrapped in paper and rags to keep it from chafing and spoiling. The back of the House looked fearful because of her.

The child was a stupid pathetic creature whom she perpetually slapped and snapped at. Through the walls we heard the smacks on his wet skin when she bathed him, each smack followed by a wail.

His pants (mother-made) had no slack; his yellow hair hung dank and lifeless; the stare in his stupid eyes alone told which way he faced. She put him out to be minded, and took a job. Every morning the no-seat little pants went slowly down the street with stilted steps. The shapeless creature stumbled and bumped into every thing, ambling half a block behind the widow who sulkily approached her job. Every step said, "I hate my job, I hate it! I married to be free! He spent my money, died, left me with *that!*"

"Come on there!"—a backward step and a crack on the yellow head.

The widow acknowledged frankly that she was not averse to a second marriage; only next time she'd see to it he had money and she would spend it.

She invited members of the Choral Society (one at a time) to come back with her "for a little music" after the Choral Practice. The child had been locked in, barricaded with furniture. She had been compelled to part with some to allow even two adults to sit by the fire comfortably. There was more than enough left. Scrambling over furniture and lowering herself to the arm of a stuffed chair, she performed, head thrown back. The window blinds were always up to the top so we could see her open mouth, stiffened back, hands beating, black eyes rolling and long horsey teeth munching the words of sentimental songs which echoed at a gallop among the jardinieres and rattled the corpulent glass front of the china cabinet.

She began at the antique shops, next she tried high-class-used, then secondhand—finally a van came and took some of the furniture to the auction rooms. It was like drawing teeth to part with it.

Now as she sang she sighed over the remaining furniture and caressed its shiny surfaces. Every visitor said he had enjoyed himself immensely, but he had so many engagments it was impossible for him to make another date.

She almost wished she had not sold the furniture. She began blaming my house, said it was not a sociable district. She fell behind in the rent, suggested I accept my rental in kind—the kind being a worn-out worthless gas range. I refused—she became abusive. I had to consult the law—that was when I popped the pail over her head and finally got her out of the House of All Sorts.

Making Musicians

I HATE pianos, tenants' pianos. They can make a landlady suffer so hideously. Lumbering tanks awaiting the touch (often unskilled) that will make them spill horrible noise, spitting it through their black and white teeth.

First the dreadful bump, bump of arrival, cruel gasps of men with backs bent—bruised and nicked woodwork—screech of rollered push-boards. Radios were a new invention then but it seemed every transient lugged around an old tin kettle of a piano.

Prospective tenants said, "You have no objection to a piano, *of course*."

"Oh, no," one lied, because one was dependent on tenants to pay mortgages and taxes.

So the piano was installed and we waited edgily till the performer operated. We did not mind child practice as much as adult jazz.

There was a sweet young girl who aspired to be a professional musician, very much in earnest, trying to unlearn previous faulty tuition. Scales rolled up and scales rolled down, noises leaped or dived or shivered out of her piano all day long. She began at 7 A.M. and laboured at it till 10 P.M. The performance took place just under my studio. Each note might have been pounded on my vertebrae. This was to go on for ever and ever—at least till the girl was made into a musician. Alas! She was very young.

Lower Westers and Doll's Flatters came to me.

"Are they permanent?"

"I am afraid so."

"The instrument is against my wall."

"It is underneath me."

There were heavy supposings "that we shall get used to it in time."

Get used to it we could not. Every day our nerves got more jangled no matter how we thundered vacuums and carpet sweepers, pots and pans. The scales boomed through every household noise.

The little girl was most persistent. When a bit of her noise went wrong she patiently repeated and repeated over and over till she won out. We were distracted.

After a fortnight we began to resign, as a nose settles down to the smell of frosted cabbage in winter. The bright spot of our day was when the little musician took her daily airing, three to four P.M.

One day we were settling to enjoy this respite when squealing wails pierced walls and floor. What torture equals a violin under the untutored hand! We realized what our peace had been when only the piano had agonized us.

The little girl did not neglect the old for the new either. For the sake of the violin she gave up her daily airing but not her piano practice.

My tenants came again. They sat down, one on either side of me.

"Yi . . . Yi . . . eee . . . ee," wailed the violin underneath us.

The tenants were as nice as possible, but it was not possible to be entirely nice. We were all agreed that the musician's family were lovely people—but—under the circumstances . . . well, something *must* be done about the circumstances. I said, "I will talk with them," but I shirked.

Days went by. I dodged past the windows of the other tenants quickly. They watched, but I just couldn't.

High note, low note, run and quiver! I drew the dust sheet over my canvas and rushed for the garden.

I went. Mother opened the door. The girl was seated at

the piano. Her pale little hands on the keyboard did not look strong, wicked or big enough to torture a whole household.

I began to talk of everything in the world except musical instruments. After a pleasant visit I sneaked back upstairs without a glance towards my tenants' windows. I sat at my easel and began to paint. Wail, wail, wail! Every wail wound me tighter. I was an eight-day clock, overwound, taut—the key would not give another turn!

I flew down the stairs.

Mother looked surprised at another visit from me so soon. Father was there and the little girl looking sweeter than ever against the curve of the rich brown violin. I turned my back so that I should not see her. Father understood. Before I got a word out he said, "I know," and nodded towards the instruments.

Sneakily I stammered, "Other tenants . . . object . . . ."

"Exactly."

Papa and Mama exchanged nods.

"Perhaps the violin practice could be arranged for where she learns."

"Impossible," said Mama.

"At the home of one of her aunts, then?"

"Both live in apartments where musical instruments are not tolerated!"

"The Park band-stand," groaned Papa with a nervous glance towards Mama. "I suggest the Park band-stand."

The little girl rushed from the room crying.

"I fear we must look for a house," said Mama.

"An isolated house," groaned Papa.

Through the open door I heard little, hurt, gasping sobs.

John's Pudding

JOHN WAS a young bachelor who for several years occupied my Doll's Flat. One Christmas his mother sent him a plum pudding from England. It travelled in a white stone-ware basin, a perfect monster of a pudding.

"Look at the thing!" John twirled it by its stained tie-down cloth. "Cost her six shillings for postage! Me out of work, *needing* underwear, socks! And *wanting* books, books, lots of books. Take the thing—three months *solid* eating."

He handed me the pudding. I shook my head. With a final twirl of the cloth he landed the pudding on the drain-board. The boy had told me of the book hints he had given Mother—of his hopes of what Christmas might bring.

"Orphanage, Salvation Army, both eat, I s'pose," he said. "I'll give 'em the dough. Want the crock? Do to feed the dogs in."

"It would not be quite fair to your mother, John. Let's give a party—feed the party pudding."

"How stomach-achey—nothing else? Who'd come?"

"Widows, spinsters, orphans. I'll get a turkey."

Lower East housed a new widow, Lower West an old widow, also her widowed daughter with a young son. My religious sister and my scholastic sister were invited, John asked his girl. All accepted. The house bubbled with activity and good smells.

We joined three tables which left just enough space for the guests to squeeze into their places. John and I sat near the kitchen door to be handy for toting dishes. There were red candles on the table, holly and apples from the garden.

My monkey, dressed in her best scarlet apron, sat warming her toes before the studio fire, all "pepped up," aware that something was going to happen. As the guests poured through the door the monkey squealed at the widows and the widows at the monkey.

The turkey had blushed his nakedness to a rosy brown and was set cross-legged and blasé in the oven doorway, a boat of gravy beside him.

When the heart of the haughty English pudding in the solid masonry of her basin had been warmed and softened by the wooing of Canadian steam, when every last thing was ready, the widows in black silk rustled into the dining-room, also my two spinster sisters with an orphan or two from the school, and John's girl.

Because of the newness of her widowhood, the East flat widow had brought for the feast a few tears as well as a dish of "foamy rolls"—"My late husband's favourites" . . . sniff! She rushed the rolls into my hands so that she could use her hankie. The seasoned widow brought loganberry wine of her own brew. The young widow brought her young son who ate too much and got sick. My religious sister brought walnuts from her own tree, and the school-marm a home-made loaf and her three orphan boarders with all diet restrictions removed for the day. John's girl was shy and talked to everybody except John. My little dogs sat on their tails—their snub noses wiggled in anticipation.

When all had trooped into the dining-room, leaving the monkey alone, she raged and jabbered. The guests poured like liquid along the narrow path into their seats, talking vivaciously about nothing, pretending they were not thinking of gone Christmases.

The turkey cut like a dream, juice trickled out as the sharp knife sliced the white breast—pink ham, turkey stuffing, green peas, potatoes mashed smooth as cream, cranberry sauce not a mite too tart. The widow's rolls melted in our mouths.

When the queenly pudding came in, attended by brandy

sauce and mounted on a blue platter, she looked like the dome of the Parliament Buildings riding the sky. Her richness oozed deliciously, spicy, fragrant, ample. The steam of her rose in superb coils as if desirous of reaching the nostrils of the widows' dead husbands. Each plated slice slid down the table, followed by a dish of brandy-sugar sauce. Everyone praised the pudding. John thought with deep affection of his mother.

When appetites were satisfied, John uncorked the widow's wine and solemnly filled all glasses, except that of my "teetotal" sister who shook her head and took her glass to the kitchen tap. We all stood up, raised our glasses to the light, admired the beauty of the wine, its clearness, its colour. We complimented the maker, yet no one drank. All seemed waiting for somebody to say something, but nobody did. Each blinked at his wine, each was thinking—the widows of their "had-beens," we spinsters of our "never materialized." John and his girl smiled their hopes into each other's eyes. We others were relics—a party of scraps and left-overs, nobody intensely related. The people of one suite shared no memories in common with those in any other.

Somebody ventured "The King." We all sipped. My "teetotal" sister choked on one of her own walnuts. The widows darted forward with kindly intended thumps.

"Water!" she spluttered, and everyone put down his wineglass to rush a water tumbler up to the choke.

"My Mother!" John raised his glass and everyone drank.

"The pudding!" I said solemnly; everyone drank again.

The monkey's patience was entirely at an end. Clank, clank, clank—the iron poker being beaten against the side of the stove. Shriek upon shriek of monkey rage!

We drank what was left of the wine quickly, put the small remnant of pudding on a tin plate, took it in to the waiting monkey and watched her eat, plum by plum, the last of John's pudding.

How Long!

HE WAS crude, enormous, coarse; his fleshy hands had fingers like bananas. You could feel their weight in the way they swung at the end of his arms.

Ridiculous that he should choose the Doll's Flat for a home while he was grinding out the life of his little third wife. She was slowly disintegrating under the grim, cruel bullying.

The Doll's Flat suited his purpose because he could keep his eye on all its rooms at once, cow her every movement crawling to do his bidding. His stare weighted her eyelids and her feet. She felt rather than heard him creeping behind with the stealth of a leery tom cat stalking a bird, never allowing it beyond the range of his seeing lest it creep aside and die before his teeth got a chance to bite into its warmth, his hand to feel the agony racing through its heart.

The great bulk of him grazed the door posts as he pushed his way from room to room. He mounted the dining table on four blocks of wood so that his huge stomach could find room beneath. I do not know whether his wife was allowed to eat standing beside him, or did she eat at the kitchen sink? His was silent cruelty. I seldom heard voices—the quiet was sinister.

The man wore glasses with thick lenses; it magnified his stare—because he was deaf, his staring was more intense.

When they went out it was he who locked the door behind them. She waited, holding his thick brutal stick. She preceded him down the stair, down the street. It must have been awful to have that heavy crunching step behind and his eyes watching, always watching. She was a meek, noise-less thing.

Bitter cold came. I stuffed the furnace to its limit, hung rugs over north windows. The hot air wouldn't face north wind, it sneaked off through south pipes.

Up and down, up and down the long outside stair I ploughed through snow which fell faster than I could sweep. During the night, snow had made the stair into one smooth glare—no treads. I shovelled a path as I descended, but the wind threw the snow back just as quickly.

The house, with the exception of the Doll's Flat, were considerate and kindly, realizing my difficulties. Every house-owner knows the agony and the anxiety regarding freeze-up and pipe bursts. Victoria's cold snaps are treach-erously irregular. Hot-air pipes are cranky. My tenants were not entirely dependent on the whims of the furnace, each suite had also an open fire and could be cosy in any weather. Nothing froze except one tap in a north bath-room, the bath of the brutal man—one hand-basin tap.

He had hot and cold in his kitchen and bath, but he roared, "This house is unfit to live in. Get a plumber *immediately.*"

I said, "That is not possible. People everywhere are without drinking-water, plumbers are racing round as fast as they can. We must manage without one hand-basin for a day or two."

The man followed me into my basement. I did not hear his footfalls in the snow. As I stooped to shovel coal his heavy fist struck across my cheek. I fell among the coal. I stumbled from basement to garden.

"House! House! how long?"

From the frozen garden I looked at it, hulking against the heavy sky.

To My Sister Alice

*I think I could turn and live with animals,
   they're so placid and self-contain'd,
I stand and look at them long and long.*
         From WALT WHITMAN'S *Song of Myself*

BOBTAILS

Kennel

THE IDEA of a Bobtail kennel did not rush into my mind with a sudden burst. It matured slowly, growing from a sincere love of and admiration for the breed, awaked by my dog, Billie, a half-bred Old English Bobtail Sheep-dog. Billie's Bobtail half was crammed with the loyalty, lovableness, wisdom, courage and kindness of the breed. His something-else half was negligible, though it debarred him from the show bench. Heart, instincts, intelligence—all were pure Bobtail.

When Billie was offered as a gift to me, I refused him, not because of his being cross-bred but because of circumstances. Billie magnificently ignored my refusal and gave himself to me in the wholesome, wholehearted way a Bobtail's devotion works. It was not the easily transferable love of a puppy, for Billie was then three years old. He had the reputation of being wicked and had several bites to his discredit.

First I bathed Billie, then I beat him for killing a chicken—this only glued his self-given allegiance to me the tighter.

He was mine for thirteen years. When he died at the age of sixteen he left such a blank that the Bobtail kennel idea, which had been rooting in me those many years, blossomed. The question was where to obtain stock. There were only a few Bobtails in Canada, brought out as "settlers' effects" from the Old Country. Their owners would as soon have thought of selling their children as their Bobtails. Some of these dogs were excellent specimens, but they were unregistered because the settlers had not bothered to enter them in the Canadian live-stock records at Ottawa, and after a generation or so had elapsed the puppies of these dogs were not eligible for registration.

After long searching I located a litter of Bobtails on a prairie farm and sent for a female puppy. I named her Loo.

Loo was a sturdy puppy of good type and the beautiful Bobtail-blue. The next step was to locate a sire. Friends of mine on a farm up-island had a Bobtail for stock work—a good dog. They mated him to a Bobtail bitch on a neighbouring farm. I never saw the so-called Bobtail mother, but the puppies from the mating were impossible. My friends gave me one.

Intelligence the pup had and a Bobtail benevolent lovableness had won him the name of "Mr. Boffin." But he had besides every point that a Bobby should not have— long nose, short, straight hair, long, impossible tail, black-and-white colour. I bred Loo to a butcher's dog, a Bobtail imported from England—well-bred, powerful, of rather coarse type but intelligent.

The butcher came to select a puppy from Loo's litter. Dangling his choice by the scruff, he said, "Work waitin', young fella. Your dad was killed last week."

The man sighed—set the pup down gently.

"Shouldn't put a pup to cattle much under a year," he said, and, looking down, saw Boffin standing beside me. Boffin had eased the dog-field gate open and come to me unbidden.

"Go back, Boffin!" I pointed to the gate. The dog immediately trotted back to his field.

"What breed is that dog?"

"Supposedly a Bobtail."

"Bobtail nothin'—I want that dog," said the butcher.

"Not for sale."

"You can't sire a Bobtail kennel by him; 'twouldn't be fair to the breed."

"Don't intend to. That dog is my wat ': and companion."

"Companion fiddlesticks! That dog wants to work. I *want* that dog."

"So do I. . . . Hen, Boffin!" I called.

From the field Boffin came and with steady gentleness persuaded the hen from the garden back into her yard.

"I want that dog," the butcher repeated and, taking Boffin's head between his hands, looked into the dog's face. "I want him for immediate work."

"He is untrained."

"He knows obedience. Instinct will do the rest. That dog is just crazy to work. Be fair to him—think it over."

I did think—but I wanted Boffin.

At dusk that night a boy came with a rope in his hand. "Come for the dog."

"What dog?"

"The one my father saw this morning—this fella I guess."

Boffin, smelling cow-barn on the boy's clothes, was leaping over him excitedly.

"We drive cattle up-island tomorrow at dawn," said the boy and threw an arm about the dog.

My Boffin, happy till then in rounding up one hen! My Boffin behind a drove of cattle! How mad—joyful he'd be! I slipped the rope through Boffin's collar, handed it to the boy. He persuaded gently. Boffin looked back at me.

"Go, Boffin!"

The smell of cow was strong, exciting his herding instincts. Boffin obeyed.

Splendid reports came of Boffin's work. I did not go to see him till six months were past, then I went. His welcome of me was overwhelming. The dog was loved and was in good shape. He stuck to my side glue-tight. We stood in the barnyard on the top of the hill. Suddenly I felt the dog's body electrify, saw his ears square. Sheep-bells sounded far off; Boffin left my side and went to that of his new master.

"Away then, Boffin!"

The man waved an arm. The dog's lean, powerful body dashed down the hill. When the dust of his violence cleared, a sea of dirty white backs was wobbling up the hill, a black-and-white quickness darting now here, now there, straightening the line, hurrying a nibbler, urging a straggler. Soberly Boffin turned his flock into their corral, went to his master for approval, then rushed to me for praise.

I was many blocks past the butcher's when I sensed following.

"Boffin!"

I had seen them shut Boffin behind a six-foot fence when I left the butcher's. The wife had said, "Father, shut Boffin in. He intends to follow."

It hurt me to return him, but I knew the job that was his birthright must prevail. . . .

Punk

LOO'S STRONG, beautiful pups found a ready market. A soldier in Victoria owned a fine Old English Bobtail Sheepdog. When he went to the war his Bobtail was desolate. I heard of the dog and went to the soldier's house, saw the shaggy huddle of misery watching the street corner around which his master had disappeared. I knocked on the house-door; the dog paid no heed, as if there was nothing now in that house that was worth guarding. A woman answered my knock.

"Yes, that is my husband's dog, 'Punk,' sulking for his master—won't eat—won't budge from watching that street corner."

A child pushed out of the door past the woman, straddled the dog's back, dug her knees into his sides and shouted, "Get up, Punk."

The dog sat back on his haunches, gently sliding the child to the ground—she lay there kicking and screaming.

"Will you sell the dog?" I asked.

"I cannot; my husband is ridiculously attached to the creature."

I told the woman about wanting to start a Bobtail kennel and my difficulty in locating a sire.

"Take Punk till my husband returns. I'd gladly be rid of the brute!"

I went to the dog. After tipping the child off he lay listless.

"Punk!"

Slowly the tired eyes turned from watching the street corner and looked at me without interest.

"He will follow no one but his master," said the woman.

The dog suffered my hand on his collar; he rose and shambled disheartenedly at my side, carrying the only luggage he possessed—his name and a broken heart.

"Punk!" Not much of a name to head a kennel! But it was the only link the dog had with his old master; he should be "Punk" still.

Loo cheered the desolation from him slowly. Me he accepted as weariness accepts rest. I was afraid to overlove Punk, for fear the woman, when she saw him washed, brushed, and handsome, might want him back. But when I took him to see her, neither dog nor woman was pleased. He followed me back to my house gladly.

Punk and Loo made a grand pair, Loo all bounce, Punk gravely dignified. They were staunchly devoted mates.

My Bobtail kennel throve; the demand for puppies was good. The government was settling returned soldiers on the land. Land must be cleared before there was much stock-work for sheep and cattle dogs. But Bobtails were comradely; they guarded the men from the desperate loneliness in those isolated places.

Punk had been with me a year. He loved Loo and he loved me; we both loved Punk. I came down the outside stair of my house one morning and found a soldier leaning over my lower landing, hands stretched out to the dogs in their field. Punk was dashing madly at the fence, leaping, backing to dash again, as breakers dash at a sea-wall. The woman who had lent me Punk and the child who had tormented him were beside the man.

"You have come for him?"—my heart sank.

The man's head shook.

"I shall be moving about. Keep him—I am glad to see him happy."

He pushed the hair back from the dog's eyes and looked into them.

"You were comfortable to think about over there, Punk." The man went quickly away.

Parting from his master did not crush Punk this time; he had Loo and he had me.

Beacon Hill

IN THE early morning the dogs burst from their sleeping quarters to bunch by the garden gate, panting for a race across Beacon Hill Park. Springs that had wound themselves tighter and tighter in their bodies all night would loose with a whirr on the opening of the garden gate. Ravenous for liberty, the dogs tore across the ball grounds at the base of Beacon Hill, slackened their speed to tag each other, wheeled back, waiting to climb the hill with me.

The top of Beacon Hill was bare. You could see north, south, east and west. The dogs rested, tongues lolling, while I looked at the new day, at the pine trees, at the sky, at the sea where it lay flat, and at the broom bushes drooped with early morning wetness. The song of the meadow-lark crumbled away the last remnants of night— three sad lingering notes followed by an exultant double chuckle that gobbled up the still-vibrating three. For one moment the morning took you far out into vague chill, but your body snatched you back into its cosiness, back to the waiting dogs on the hill top. They could not follow out there, their world was walled, their noses trailed the earth. What a dog cannot hear or smell he distrusts; unless objects are close or move he does not observe them. His nature is to confirm what he sees by his sense of sound or of smell.

"Shut that door! Shut that door!" staccato and dictatorial shouted the voice of the quail as they scuttled in single file from side to side of the path, feet twinkling and slick bodies low-crouched. The open-mouthed squawks of gulls spilled over the sea. From behind the Hill came the long resentful cry of the park peacock, resentful because, having attained supreme loveliness, he could push his magnificence no further.

Pell-mell we scampered down the hillside. A flat of green land paused before letting its steepness rush headlong down clay cliffs. The sea and a drift-piled beach were below. Clay paths meandered down the bank. They were slippery; to keep from falling you must lodge your feet among the grass hummocks at the path-side. The dogs hurled their steady four-footed shapes down the steepness, and awaited me on the pebbly beach. Sea-water wet their feet, wind tossed their hair, excitement quivered in every fibre of their aliveness.

On our return the house was waking. The dogs filed soberly under yet blinded windows, mounted three steps to the landing, sank three steps to the garden, passed into their play-field, earnest guardians of our house. I went to my daily tasks.

Whenever the Bobbies heard my step on the long outside stair, every body electrified. Tongues drew in, ears squared, noses lifted. The peer from all the eyes under all the bangs of crimpy hair concentrated into one enormous "looking," riveted upon the turning of the stair where I would first show. When I came they trembled, they danced and leapt with joy, scarcely allowing me to squeeze through the gate, crowding me so that I had to bury my face in the crook of an arm to protect it from their ardent lickings, their adoring Bobtail devotion.

The Garden

THE GARDEN was just ordinary—common flowers, everyday shrubs, apple-trees. Like a turbulent river the Bobtails raced among gay flowers and comfortable shrubs on their way from sleeping-pen to play-field, a surge of grey movement weaving beautiful patterns among poppy, rose, delphinium, whose flowers showed more brilliantly colourful for the grey intertwistings of shaggy-coated dogs among them.

In the centre of the lawn grew a great cherry-tree better at blossoming than at fruiting. To look into the heart of the cherry-tree when it was blossoming was a marvel almost greater than one could bear. Millions and millions of tiny white bells trembling, swaying, too full of white holiness to ring. Beneath the cherry-tree the Bobbies danced—bounding, rebounding on solid earth, or lying flat in magnificent relaxation.

East, west, north the garden was bounded by empty lots; its southern limit was the straight square shadow of my apartment house.

The depth and narrowness of my lot made the height above it seem higher, a height in which you could pile dreams up, up until the clouds hid them.

Sunday

RELIGIOUS people did not know more precisely which day was Sunday than did my Bobtails. On Sunday the field gate stood open. Into the garden trooped a stream of grey vitality, stirring commotion among the calm of the flowers. The garden's Sunday quiet fastened almost immediately upon the dogs. In complete abandon their bodies stretched upon the grass, flat as fur rugs. You could scarcely tell which end of a dog was head and which tail, both were so heavily draped in shagginess. At the sound of my voice one end lifted, the other wobbled. Neither could you tell under the mop over his eyes whether the dog slept or woke—in sleep he was alert; awake, he was dignified, intent.

When Sunday afternoon's quiet was broken by five far-off strokes of the town clock, we all sprang for the basement. In the entrance hall was a gas-ring; on it stood a great stew-pot. There was also a tap and a shelf piled with dinner pans. The dogs ranged themselves along the basement wall, tongues drawn in, ears alert. I took the big iron spoon and served from the stew-pot into the dinner pans. As I served I sang—foolish jingles into which I wove each dog's name, resonant, rounded, full-sounding. Each owner at the sound of his own name bounced and wobbled—waiting, taut, hoping it would come again.

The human voice is the strongest thing a dog knows—it can coax, terrify, crush. Words are not meaning to a dog. He observes the lilt, the tone, the music—anger and rebuke have meaning too and can crush him. I once had a stone-deaf dog and once I had one that was stone-blind. The deaf dog had nothing to respond to but the pat of pity. She could only "watch"; at night her world was quite blank. The blind dog's blackness was pictured with sounds and with smells. He knew night-scents and night-sounds from day-scents and day-sounds; he heard the good-natured scuffle of dog-play, barkings, rejoicings; he heard also the voice of the human being he loved. The blind dog's *listening* life was happy. The deaf's dog only happiness was to be held close and warm—to feel.

Puppy Room

THE PUPPY room in the basement brimmed with youngness,
with suckings, cuddlings, lickings, squirmings—puppies
whose eyes were sealed against seeing, puppies whose ears
were sealed against hearing for the first ten days of life,
puppies rolling around in their mother's box like sausages,
heavy in the middle and with four legs foolishly sticking
out sideways, rowing aimlessly and quite unable to support
the weight of their bodies.

Some Bobtails are born entirely tailless, some have tails
which are docked at the age of three days, some have
stumps, some twists.

Loo was never happy with a new family until she had
brought Punk in to inspect it. Punk lumbered behind his
mate, nosed into her box, sniffed and ambled out again,
rather bored. It satisfied Loo. The other Bobtail mothers
never brought Punk to see their families, but Loo was
Punk's favourite mate.

Bobbies have large families—nine is an ordinary litter.
Once Flirt had fourteen pups at one birth. I never allowed
a mother to raise more than six pups unaided. If the demand was good I kept more, but I went round the family
three times a day with a feeding bottle so that all the pups
were satisfied and my mothers not overtaxed. One spring
thirty pups were born in the kennel nursery within one
week. It took me three hours a day for three weeks "bot-
tling" pups, but they throve amazingly. Sometimes a pup was
stubborn and would not take the bottle; then I tickled him
under the chin; this made him yawn and I popped the
bottle into his yawn and held it there till he sucked. The

mothers watched me with great interest; my yawn method was a joke between us. They were most grateful for my help, those patient, loving dog mothers.

Poison

THE BUTCHER lifted half a pig's head to his nose, sent it flying with a disgusted hurl into the bundle of scrap that Bobtail Meg was waiting to carry home in her saddle-bags for the kennel. Meg loved to lug the butcher-scraps home for me. When her saddle-bags were filled Meg rose, shook butcher-floor sawdust from her coat and waddled the bones away with pompous pride. Meg never was so happy as when she was busy.

There was something sinister in that pig's one eye when I stuck his half-head into the dog-pot. It made the soup into a rich, thick jelly and smelled good.

Flirt, Loo's daughter, had a litter two weeks old. Flirt was ravenous and gobbled a generous portion of soup and meat. The next day a pup was sick, others were ailing. The veterinary ran a stubby finger around the sick pup's gums. "Teething," he said, and, taking a pocket knife, slashed the pup's gums, wiped the knife on his pants and rammed it into his pocket along with my two dollars. That night the pup died. I was furious—puppies never bothered over teething! I called another veterinary. "Poison," said the old man, and I remembered the butcher's nose and the pig's eye. This vet shook his head and killed the sickest pup to prove his diagnosis by post mortem. He said, "This is a matter for nursing not doctoring. I think all of them will die."

Every pup was bespoken. I did not want them to die and the pups wanted to live—they put up a good fight and won.

I took them away from Flirt. They were too listless to

suck a bottle. I spooned brandy and milk down their throats, and to the amazement of the veterinary reared the entire litter. The runt was the grittiest pup of all; for days he writhed out of one convulsion into the next—calmed from one only to go through it all over again. One morning before dawn I found him stiff, tongue lolling, eyes glazed. I had for several days *almost* decided to put an end to his misery. From force of habit I trickled brandy over the lolling tongue—no response. A grave to dig in the morning! Dazed with tiredness I put the pup into his basket and went back to the garden room where I was sleeping during the poison trouble so that I might watch over the puppies. Sticking basket and feeding-bottle into a far corner of the room I tumbled into bed.

The sun and a queer noise woke me. I peeped overboard to see the runt seated on the floor in a patch of sunshine, the feeding-bottle braced between his paws, sucking with feeble fury.

I cried, "You gritty little beast!", warmed his milk and a hot-water bottle, tucked him into his basket and named him "Grits."

Grits turned into a fine and most intelligent dog. He was sold and sent as a love-gift to a man's sweetheart in Bermuda. Another of that poisoned litter went to France, pet of a wealthy man's children; another to Hollywood, where he saved two children from drowning while sea bathing. He was filmed. But mostly my Bobbies homed themselves in Canada. They won in the local dog shows. I did not show them further afield. To raise prize-winners was not the objective of my kennel. I aimed at producing healthy, intelligent working stock and selling puppies at a price the man of moderate means could afford, yet keeping the price high enough to insure the buyer feeling that his *money's worth* must be given due care and consideration.

Naming

EVERY creature accepting domesticity is entitled to a name.

It enraged me to find, perhaps a year later, that a pup I had sold was adult and unnamed, or was just called "Pup," "Tyke," or some general name. Were humans so blind that a creature's peculiarities suggested no name special to him? —nothing but a *class* tag? In selling a young pup, the naming was always left to the buyer. If I raised or half-raised a dog, I named him. For my kennel I liked the patriarchs—Noah, Moses, David, Adam. They seemed to suit the grey-bearded, rugged dignity of the Bobbies whose nature was earnest, faithful, dutiful.

At dog shows kennel-men smiled at the names on my entries. They said, "Why not 'Prince,' 'Duke,' 'King'?— more aristocratic!" But I clung to my patriarchs. The Old English Bobtail Sheep-dog is more patriarch than aristocrat.

Meg the Worker

BOBTAIL MEG was registered. I bought her by mail; I sent the money but no dog came. After writing a number of letters which were not answered, I applied to a lawyer. He wrote—Meg came. Her seller claimed that the dog had been run over on the way to be shipped. She was a poor lank creature with a great half-healed wound in her side. I was minded to return her. Then I saw the look in Meg's eyes, the half-healed, neglected wound, and I could not send her back to the kind of home she had obviously come from. I saw too how ravenously she ate, how afraid she was to accept kindness, how distrustful of coaxing.

Her coat was a tangled mass, barbed with last year's burs, matted disgustingly with cow dung. Before I let her go among my own dogs, she had to be cleaned. I got a tub and a pair of shears. When the filth was cleared away Meg shook herself; her white undercoat fluffed patchily, she looked chewed but felt clean and was eased by the dressing of her wound. She felt light-hearted, too, and self-respecting. Before the shears had finished their job Meg had given me her heart.

The kennel accepted Meg; Meg had no ears or eyes for any living thing, beast or human, but me. All day she sat in the dog-field, her eyes glued to my windows or the stair, waiting trembling to hear my step, to see my shadow pass.

When her coat grew Meg did not look too bad. She was very intelligent and had been taught to work. Idleness irked Meg; her whole being twitched to obey; her eyes pleaded, "Work!" On Beacon Hill she bustled in and out among the broom hunting imaginary sheep and would slink shamedly to my heel when she failed to find any.

I invented work for Meg. I was clearing the smaller stones off the far field, Meg following my every trip to a far corner where I emptied my basket. I stitched a pair of saddle-bags and bound them on to Meg. The dog stood patiently while I filled them with small stones and then trotted them to the dumping place proudly. I took her and her saddle-bags to the butcher's for the daily kennel rations. Meg lugged them home, nose high when she passed the dog-field where the others sniffed enviously. The bone that was her reward did not please Meg much, she let the others take if from her. Had any of them taken her job, Meg's heart would have been broken.

A kind-voiced man rushed into the kennel one day.

"I want a trained cattle-dog to take with me to the Cariboo immediately!"

He fancied Meg; I liked the way he handled her. I let Meg go to the big spaces and the job that was hers by right.

Basement

CREEPING around a basement in the small dark hours is not cheerful. A house's underneathness is crushing—weight of sleep pressing from the flats above, little lumps of coal releasing miniature avalanches which rattle down the black pile, furnace grimly dead, asbestos-covered arms prying into every corner.

Just inside the basement door was a yawn of black. This portion of basement was uncemented, low-ceiled, earthy, unsunned. Often in daytime I must creep here among the cobwebs to feel hot-air-pipes and see that each tenant got his just amount of heat. Ghastly white pipes twisted and meandered through the dimness. A maple stump was still rooted here. Every year it sprouted feebler, paler shoots, anaemic, ghastly! Punk kept bones under the hollow of this old root. At night when we went down to tend puppies or sick dogs I scuttled quickly past the black. Cobwebby darkness did not worry Punk; he dashed in and dug up a bone to gnaw while I tended puppies.

Night

MANY A winter night Punk, who slept upstairs in my flat, and I crept down the long outside stair to the basement, sometimes crunching snow on every step, sometimes slipping through rain. Old moon saw us when she was full. When new, her chin curled towards her forehead and she did not look at us. The corners of the stairway were black. Sometimes we met puffs of wind, sometimes wreaths of white mist. It was comfortable to rest a hand on Punk, envying his indifference to dark, cold, fear. I envied Punk his calm acceptance of everything.

The Dog-Thief

I LOVED sleeping in the garden room, my garden room where flowers and creatures were so close.

It was nearly time for the moon to turn in and for me to turn out. Punk, lying on the mat beside my bed, got up, crept to the open door—stood, a blurred mass of listening shadow.

The blind man in my downstairs flat had twice before told me of rustlings in the dog-field at night. His super-sensitiveness had detected fingers feeling along the outer wall of his flat.

"I think," he had suggested, "that someone is after a pup."

I threw on a gown and stood beside Punk. The shadow by the pup-house door looked, I thought, unusually bulky. Punk and I went down the cinder path. Punk growled, the shadow darted behind the lilac bush, uttering a high sing-song squeal. There was light enough to show Chinese cut of clothes—I heard the slip-slop of Chinese shoes.

"What do you want?"

"Me loosed," he whined.

"You are not lost. You came in by my gate. Put him out, Punk!"

Whites of slant, terrified eyes rolled as the dog allowed him to pass but kept at his heels until he was out in the street. Whoever bribed that Chinaman to steal a pup had not reckoned on Punk's being loose, nor had he counted on my sleeping in my garden.

Selling

A STRANGER stood at the garden gate. Young dogs leapt, old dogs stiffened and growled, enquiring noses smelled through the bars of the gate at the head of the garden steps. Fore-paws rested a step higher than hind-paws, making dogs' slanted bodies, massed upon the steps, look like a grey thatch. Strong snuffing breaths were drawn in silently, expelled loudly.

I came into the middle of the dog pack and asked of the stranger, "You wanted something?"

The man bracketed dogs and me in one disdainful look. "I want a dog."

The coarse hand that swept insolently over the dogs' heads enraged them. They made such bedlam that an upper and a lower tenant's head protruded from the side of the house, each at the level of his own flat.

"What price the big brute?"—indicating Punk.

"Not for sale."

"The blue bitch?"—pointing to Loo.

"Not for sale."

"Anything for sale?" he sneered.

"Puppies."

"More bother'n they're worth! . . . G'ar on!"

He struck Punk's nose for sniffing at his sleeve.

"D'you want to sell or d'you not?"

"Not."

The man shrugged—went away.

Money in exchange for Bobbies was dirty from hands like those.

Kipling

THE DOGS and I were Sundaying on the garden lawn. Suddenly every dog made a good-natured rush at the garden gate. A man and a woman of middle age were leaning over it. The dogs bunched on the steps below the gate. The woman stretched a kindly hand to them. The man only stared—stared and smiled.

"Were you looking for somebody?" I asked.

"Not exactly—he," the woman waved a hand towards the man, "has always had a notion for Bobtails."

I invited them into my garden.

"Would you like to see the pups?" I said, and led the way to the puppy pen. The woman leant across, but the man jumped over the low fence and knelt on the earth among the puppies.

"Your 'Sunday,' Father!" reminded the woman.

He gave a flip to his dusty knees, but continued kneeling among scraping, pawing pups. Picking up a sturdy chap, he held it close.

"Kip, Kip," he kept saying.

"Kipling and Bobtails is his only queerness," the woman apologized.

"I suppose they are very expensive?" the man said, putting the puppy down on the ground. To the pup he said, "You are not a necessity, little fellow!" and turned away.

"There's times *wants* is *necessities*, Father," said the woman. "You go ahead and pick. Who's ate them millions and millions of loaves you've baked these thirty years? Not you. Jest time it is that you took some pleasure to yourself. Pick the best, too!"

With shaking hand the baker lifted the pup he had held before, the one he had already named Kip. He hurried the puppy's price out of his pocket (Ah! He had known he was going to buy!), crooked one arm to prevent the pup from slipping from beneath his coat, crooked the other arm for his wife to take hold. Neither of them noticed the dust on his "Sundays" as they smiled off down the street.

Sales like this were delicious—satisfactory to buyer, seller, dog.

Lorenzo Was Registered

ONLY ONCE did I come upon a Bobbie who was a near-fool; he was a dog I bought because of his registration, for I went on coveting registration for my dogs. Lorenzo was advertised: "A magnificent specimen of the noble breed—registered name—'Lorenzo.'" He was impressive enough on paper; in the flesh he was a scraggy, muddle-coloured, sparse-coated creature, with none of the massive, lumbering shagginess of the true Bobbie. His papers apparently were all right. His owner described the dog as "an ornament to any *gentleman's* heel." I wanted dignity of registration for my kennels, not ornament for my heels.

Lorenzo had acquired an elegant high-stepping gait in place of the Bobtail shamble, also a pernickety appetite. He scorned my wholesome kennel fare, toothing out dainties and leaving the grosser portions to be finished by the other dogs.

Lorenzo was mine for only a short time. I had a letter asking for a dog of his type from a man very much the type of Lorenzo's former owner. The letter said, "I have a fancy for adding an Old Country note to my Canadian farm in the shape of an Old English Bobtail Sheep-dog. I have no stock to work, but the dog must be a good heeler —registration *absolutely necessary*."

High-stepping Lorenzo was in tune with spats and a monocle, was registered and a good heeler. I told the man I had better-type dogs unregistered, but a check came by return emphatically stating that Lorenzo was the dog for him.

Lorenzo's buyer declared himself completely satisfied with foolish, high-stepping, bad-typed Lorenzo—Lorenzo was registered.

Sissy's Job

THE EARTH was fairly peppered with David Harbin's cousins. No matter what part of the world was mentioned David said, "I have a cousin out there." David was a London lawyer. During law vacation he visited cousins all over the world. He always came to see me when visiting Canadian cousins.

David and I were sitting on my garden bench talking. David said, "My last visit (to a Canadian cousin) has left me very sad. Cousin Allan and I were brought up together; his parents died and my Mother took Allan. He was a deaf-mute. His dumbness did not seem to matter when we were boys. We used dumb language and were jolly. When Allan had to face life, to take his dumbness out into the world, that was different—he bought a ranch in Canada, a far-off, isolated ranch. Now he is doubly solitary, surrounded by empty space as well as dead silence."

While David talked a Mother Bobtail came and laid her chin on his knee. His hand strayed to her head but he did not look at her. His seeing was not in the garden; it was back on the lonely ranch with dumb Allan. The dog sensed trouble in David's voice, in his touch she felt sadness. She leapt, licked his face! David started.

"Down, Sissy," I called.

But David shouted, "Dog, *you're* the solution. Is she for sale?"

"Sissy," I said, "was intended for a kennel matron. But she was temperamental over her first litter, did not mother them well. She will do better next time perhaps, unless. . . ."

I caught David's eye . . . .

"Unless I send her over to mother dumb Allan!"

David fairly danced from my garden, he was so happy in his solution for Allan's loneliness.

From England he wrote, "Allan's letters have completely changed, despondency gone from them. Bless Bobtails!—Sissy did it."

Min the Nurse

IN THE public market the butcher's scale banged down with a clank. The butcher grinned first at the pointer, then at me. The meat on the scale was worth far more than I was paying.

"Bobtails," murmured the butcher caressingly—"Bobtails is good dogs! . . . 'Member the little 'un I bought from your kennel a year back?"

"I do. Hope she turned out well—good worker?"

"Good worker! You bet. More sick nurse than cattle driver. Our Min's fine! Y'see, Missus be bed-fast. Market days she'd lay there, sun-up to sun-down, alone. I got Min; then she wan't alone no more; Min took hold. Market days Min minds wife, Min minds farm, Min keeps pigs out of potatoes, Min guards sheep from cougars, Min shoos coon from hen-house—Min, Min, Min. Min runs the whole works, Min do!"

He leaned a heavy arm across the scale, enraging its spring. He wagged an impressive forefinger and said, "Females understands females." Nod, nod, another nod, "Times there's no easin' the frets of Missus. Them times I off's to barn. 'Min,' I sez, 'You stay,' an' Min stays. Dogs be powerful understandin'."

He handed me the heavy parcel and gave yet another nod.

"Fido's chop, butcher!"

The voice was overbearing and tart; then it crooned down to the yapping, blanketed, wriggling "Pom" under her arm, "Oo's chopsie is coming, ducksie!"

The butcher slammed a meagre chop on the scale, gathered up the corners of the paper, snapped the string, flung the package over the counter, tossed the coin into his cash box—then fell to sharpening knives furiously.

Babies

THE DOGS and I were absorbing sultry calm under the big maple tree in their play-field. They sprawled on the parched grass, not awake enough to seek trouble, not asleep enough to be unaware of the slightest happening.

A most extraordinary noise was happening, a metallic gurgle that rasped in even-spaced screeches. The noise stopped at our gate; every dog made a dash. Punk and Loo, who had been sitting on top of the low kennel against which I rested, leaped over my head to join the pack. The fence of their field angled the front gate. A weary woman shoved the gate open with the front wheels of the pram she pushed. A squeal or two and the noise stopped.

The woman drove the baby-carriage into the shade of the hawthorn tree and herself slumped on to the bench just inside my gate. Her head bobbed forward; she was so asleep that even the dogs' barking in her ear and pushing her hat over one eye, pawing and sniffing over the fence against which the bench backed, did not wake her. For a few seconds her hand went on jogging the pram, then dropped to her side like a weighted bag. I called the dogs back and every soul of us drowsed out into the summer hum. Only the sun was really awake. He rounded the thorn-tree and settled his scorch on to the baby's nose.

The child squirmed. He was most unattractive, a speckle-faced, slobbery, scowling infant. A yellow turkish-towelling bib under his chin did not add to his beauty. In the afternoon glare he looked like a sunset. He rammed a doubled-up fist into his mouth and began to gnaw and grumble. The woman stirred in her unlovely sleep, and her hand started automatically to jog the pram handle. I had come from the dog field and was sitting beside her on the bench. Eyes peering from partly stuck-together lids like those of a nine-day-old kitten, she saw me.

"Teethin'," she yawned, and nodded in the direction of the pram; then her head flopped and she resumed loose-lipped, snorting slumber.

"Wa-a-a-a!"

The dogs came inquisitively to the fence.

"'Ush, 'Ush!"

She saw the dogs, felt their cool noses against her cheek.

"Where be I?—Mercy! I come for a pup! *That's* where I be! 'Usband says when we was changin' shifts walkin' son last night. 'Try a pup, Mother,' 'e sez—'We've tried rattles an' balls an' toys. Try a live pup to soothe 'is frettiness.' So I come. 'Usband sez, 'Git a pup same age as son'—Sooner 'ave one 'ouse-broke me'self—wot yer got?"

"I have pups three months old."

"Ezzact same age as son! Bring 'em along."

She inspected the puppy, running an experienced finger around his gums.

"Toothed a'ready! 'E'll do."

She tucked the pup into the pram beside the baby who immediately seized the dog's ear and began to chew. The pup as immediately applied himself greedily to the baby's bottle and began to suck.

"Well, I never did!" said the mother. "Let 'im finish—'ere's a comfort for son."

She dived into a deep cloth bag.

"That pup was brought up on a bottle," I explained.

"That so? Tote!" she commanded. I operated the pram's screech till the comfort was in the baby's mouth and the pup paid for.

Loo and I, watching, heard the pram-full of baby whine down the street. Loo, when satisfied that the noise was purely mechanical, not puppy-made, shook herself and trotted contentedly back to the field—finished with that lot of puppies. Nature would now rest Loo, prepare her for

the next lot of puppies. Life, persistent life! Always pushing, always going on.

Distemper

DISTEMPER swooped upon the kennel. Dance went from strong, straight legs leaving trembling weakness. Noses parched, cracked with fever, eyes crusted, ears lay limp; there were no tailless, all-over wobbles of joy, anticipation, curiosity; dinners went untouched.

One veterinary advocated open air and cold, the other sweating in a steam-box. I tried every distemper remedy then known. Death swept the kennel. A bucket of water stood always ready beside the garden tap for the little ones. When convulsions set in, I put an end to the pup's suffering. After convulsions started the case was hopeless.

These drowning horrors usually had to be done between midnight and dawn. The puppies yelped in delirium. (Tenants must not be disturbed by dog agony.) In the night-black garden I shook with the horror of taking life—when it must be done, the veterinary destroyed adult dogs that could not recover.

That bout of distemper took the lives of fifteen of my Bobtails, and took two months to do it in. Creena, a beautiful young mother dog I had just bought, was the last adult to die. The vet took her body away; there was room for no more graves in my garden. Two half-grown dead pups in dripping sacks lay in the shed waiting for dark—of Loo's eight puppies (the ones the Prince of Wales had admired and fondled in the Victoria show a few weeks earlier) only two were left; they were ramping around their box in delirium. I could endure no more. It might be several days yet before they died. I took them to the garden bucket.

148

Now the kennel was empty except for Loo, Punk and Flirt. We must start all over again. That night when dark came I heaped four dripping sacks into the old pram, in which I brought bones from the butcher's, and trundled my sad load through black, wild storm to the cliffs off Beacon Hill. Greedy white breakers licked the weighted sacks from my hands, carried them out, out.

Punk waited at home. The tragedy in the kennel he did not comprehend—trouble of the human being he loved distressed the dog sorely. Whimpering, he came close— licked my hands, my face for sorrow.

Gertie

THE MAN said, "The garden belongs to my cousins, I board with them."

I could see he minded being only a "boarder," minded having no ground-rights.

The resentful voice continued, "Gertie has outgrown her pen and her welcome."

Pulling a stalk of wild grass, he chewed on it furiously. This action, together with the name of the dog, made me remember the man. A year ago he had come to my kennel. I had been impressed with the hideousness of the name "Gertie" for a dog. He had looked long at Loo's pups, suddenly had swooped to gather a small female that was almost all white into his arms. "This one!" he exclaimed, "daintiest pup of them all!" and, putting his cheek against the puppy, he murmured, "Gertie your name is, Gertie, *Gertie!*" Then he tucked her inside his coat and went sailing down the street, happy.

Now Gertie was up for sale and I was buying her back.

With a squeezing burst Gertie shot through her small door to fling herself upon her master. We stood beside the outgrown pen.

"I made it as big as the space they allowed would permit," giving a scornful glance at the small quarters of the big dog. "All right when she was little. Now it is cruel to keep a creature of her size in it."

Gertie was circling us joyously. Her glad free yelps brought the cousins rushing from their house, one lady furnished with a broom, the other with a duster. One dashed to the pansy-bed waving the duster protectively.

The other broomed, militant, at the end of the delphinium row.

"Leash her!" squealed Pansy.

"Leash her!" echoed Delphinium.

The man took a lead from his pocket and secured Gertie. The women saw me take the lead in my hand, saw me put Gertie's price into his. He dashed the money into his pocket without a look, as if it burned his hand to hold it, turned abruptly, went into the house. The duster and the broom limped. The women smiled.

"Destructive and clumsy as a cow!" said Pansy, and scowled as Gertie passed them on her way to the gate, led by me.

"Creatures that size should be banned from city property!" agreed Delphinium with a scowl the twin of Pansy's.

Gertie, her head turned back over her shoulder, came with me submissively to the gate; here she sat down, would not budge. I pushed her out on to the pavement and shut the gate behind her—neither coaxing nor shoving would get Gertie further.

Suddenly there was a quick step on the garden walk—Gertie sprang, waiting for the gate to open, waiting to fling herself upon her adored master, pleading. I let go the lead, busied myself examining blight on the hedge. I was positive the sun had glittered on some unnatural shininess on the man's cheek. He handed me Gertie's lead. "I shall not come to see her. Will you give her the comfort of retaining the sound of her old name? Gertie," he whispered, "Gertie!" and the dog waggled with joy.

Gertie! Ugh, I *loathed* the name—Gertie among my patriarchs!

I said, "Yes, I'll keep the sound."

He commanded, "Go, Gertie."

The dog obeyed, rising to amble unenthusiastically in the direction of his pointing finger and my heels.

Honestly, I "Gertied" Gertie all the way home. Then, taking her head between my hands and bending close said, "Flirtie, Flirtie, Flirtie," distinctly into the dog's ear. She was intelligent and responded just as well to "Flirtie" as to "Gertie." After all, I told myself, it was the *sound* I promsed that Gertie should keep.

The "ie" I gradually lopped off too. Maybe her master had abbreviated to "Gert" sometimes. Flirt became one of the pillars of my kennel.

She was frightened to death of her first puppies. She dug holes in the earth and buried them as soon as they were born. I dug the pups up, restored them to life, but Flirt refused to have anything to do with them. In despair I brought old Loo into the next pen and gave the pups to her. She bathed and cuddled them all day. More she could not do as she had no puppies of her own at that time. At evening when the pups squealed with hunger and Loo was just a little bored, I sat an hour in Flirt's pen reasoning with her. Little by little the terrified, trembling mother allowed her puppies to creep close, closer, finally to touch her.

Her realization of motherhood came with a rush. She gave herself with Bobtail wholeheartedness to her pups, and ever after was a genuine mother.

The Cousins' Bobtails

TWO MEN, cousins, came to buy Bobtails. One cousin was rich and had a beautiful estate; the other was poor and was overseer and cowman for his cousin.

The rich cousin bought the handsomest and highest-priced pup in the kennel. After careful consideration the poor man chose the runt of the litter.

"This pup has brains," he said.

A chauffeur carried the rich man's pup to his car. The poor man, cuddling his puppy in his arm, walked away smiling.

A year later the rich cousin came to see me. He said, "I am entering my Bobtail in the show. I would like you to look him over." He sent his car and I went to his beautiful estate. His dog, Bob, was Loo's pup, well-mannered, handsome. I asked how the dog was for work.

"Well, our sheep are all show-stock, safely corralled. There *is* no work for Bob except to be ornamental. The women folks are crazy about him, never allow him 'round the barns. My cousin's dog does our cattle work."

We went to the cattle-barns, Bob walking behind us with dignity. The cow-cousin and a burly Bobtail were bringing in the dairy herd. They gave a nod and a "woof" in our direction and continued about their business. When the cows were stalled the man said "Right, Lass!" and man and dog came to where we stood. Wisps of straw stuck in the work-dog's coat, mud was on her feet, she reeked of cow. She stood soberly beside her master paying no heed either to Bob or to us.

"She handles the cows well," I said to the cow-cousin.

"Wouldn't trade Lass for a kingdom!" He directed a scornful eye and a pointing finger towards Bob, muttering, "Soft as mush!"

"Are you entering Lass in the show?"

"Show Lass! Lass has no time to sit on show-benches—on her job from dawn till dark—cows, pigs, hens. Leghorn fowls are pretty flighty you know, but Lass can walk into the midst of a flock—no fuss, just picks out the hen of my pointing, pins the bird to the ground by placing her paw squarely but gently on its back, holds on till I come. She can separate hens from pullets, cajoling each into their right pens—off then to the bushes for those tiresome youngsters that *will* roost in the trees. No peace for bird or beast 'round this farm unless it obeys Lass!"

Bob went to the show. He won "the blue," delighting in the fuss and admiration. Lass at home commanded her pigs, drove hens, plodded after cows, but no fluttering ribbon of blue on Lass's collar could have exalted her Bobtail pride as did "Good girl, Lass!"—her master's voice, her master's praise.

Blue or Red

HER SKIN was like rag ill-washed and rough-dried. Both skin and clothing of the woman were the texture of hydrangea blossoms—thin, sapless. On exaggeratedly high heels her papery structure tottered.

"I want a dog."

"Work dog or companion?"

"One-o-them whatcher-callum—the kind you got."

"Bobtail Sheep-dogs."

"I ain't got no sheep, jest a husband. Lots younger'n me. I tried to keep my years down to his—can't be done,"—she shrugged.

The shrug nearly sent her thin shoulder blades ripping through the flimsy stuff of her blouse. She gripped a puppy by the scruff, raised him to eye-level, giggled, shook the soft, dangling lump lovingly, then lowered him to her flat chest. She dug her nose into his wool as if he had been a powder puff, hugging till he whimpered. She put him on the ground, rummaged in a deep woollen bag.

The money was all in small coin, pinches here and pinches there hoarded from little economies in dress and housekeeping. When the twenty-five and fifty-cent pieces, the nickels and the dimes were in neat piles on the garden bench, she counted them three times over, picked up her pup and went away. The silly heels tap-tapped down the garden path. She gave backward nods at the little piles of coin on the bench, each coin might have been a separate lonesomeness that she was saying goodbye to, grateful that they had brought her this wriggling happy thing to love.

A year later I was working in my garden and the little hydrangea person came again. Beside her lumbered a massive Bobtail. When he saw his brethren in the field his excitement rose to a fury of prances and barkings.

"Down, Jerry, down!"

No authority was in the voice. The dog continued to prance and to bark.

"Must a dog on the show bench be chained?"

"Most certainly he must be chained."

"That settles it! Jerry, Jerry, I *did* so want you to win the blue!"

"He is fine," I said.

"Couldn't be beaten, but Jerry will neither chain nor leash!"

"He could easily be taught."

"I dare not; Jerry is powerful. I'd be afraid."

I took a piece of string from my pocket, put it through Jerry's collar, engaged his attention, led him down the garden and back. He led like a lamb.

"See." I gave the string into her hand. The dog pulled back, breaking the string the moment her thin uncertain grasp took hold.

"Leave Jerry with me for half an hour."

She looked dubious.

"You won't beat him?"

"That would not teach him."

Reluctantly she went away. Jerry was so occupied in watching the dogs in the field he did not notice that she was gone. I got a stout lead, tied Jerry to the fence, then I took Flirt and Loo to the far field and ran them up and down. Jerry wanted to join in the fun. When he wanted hard enough I coupled him to Flirt. We all raced. Jerry was mad with the fun of it. Then I led him alone. By the time the woman came back Jerry understood what a lead was. He was reluctant to stop racing and go with his mistress. I saw them head for home, tapping heels and fluttering drapes, hardly able to keep up with the vigorous Jerry.

Jerry took his place on the show-bench and chained all right, but, in the show ring, his mistress had no control over him. He and his litter brother were competing, having outclassed all entries. Bob, Jerry's competitor, was obedient, mannerly. The Judge turned to take the red and the blue ribbons from the table, the frown of indecision not quite gone. Blue ribbon in right hand, red in left, he advanced. Jerry was flying for the far end of the ring, leash swinging. His mistress was dusting herself after a roll in the sawdust. The Judge handed the blue ribbon to Bob's master, to the hydrangea lady he gave the red. Bob's master fixed the blue to Bob's collar, the red ribbon dangled in the limp hand of Jerry's mistress. She did not care whether its redness fell among the sawdust and was lost or not—her Jerry was beaten!

Decision

PUNK IN his prime was siring magnificent puppies, but I had to think forward. Punk and Loo, the founders of my kennel, would one day have to be replaced by young stock. Bobbies are a long-lived breed. Kennel sires and matrons, however, must not be over old if the aim of the kennel is to produce vigorous working stock. It was time I thought about rearing a young pair to carry on.

I had a beautiful puppy, a son of Punk's, named David. I had also a fine upstanding puppy of about the same age that I had imported from the prairies and named Adam. In points there was little to choose between the youngsters, both were excellent specimens and promised well. I watched their development with interest. The pups were entirely different in disposition; they were great chums. David was gentle, calm—Adam bold, rollicking. David's doggy brain worked slow and steady. Adam was spontaneous—all fire. He had long legs and could jump a five-foot fence with great ease. If Adam did not know my exact whereabouts he leapt and came to find me; David lay by the gate patiently waiting, eyes and ears alert for the least hint.

From early puppyhood Adam dominated David; not that David was in any way a weakling, but he adored Adam and obeyed him. Their pens were adjacent. At feeding time Adam bolted his dinner and then came to the dividing partition. David, a slower eater, was only half through his meal, but when Adam came and stood looking through the bars, David pushed his own food dish, nosing it close to Adam's pen. Adam shoved a paw under the boards and clawed the dish through to finish the food that was David's. This happened day after day; there was deliberate uncanny understanding between the two dogs—David always giving, Adam always taking.

One day I was housecleaning and could not have too many dogs under my feet. I shut them all into the playfield, all except David who lay on the lawn quietly watching my coming and going. Young Adam leapt the fence in search of me. Taking him to the far field I chained him and chained Eve at his side for company.

When it began to rain I was too busy to notice, and by the time I went into the garden to shake some rugs everything was soaking wet.

"Oh, poor Adam and Eve!" I exclaimed. "Chained in the open without shelter!"

I went to put them into the shed. To my amazement I found Adam and Eve each cuddled down on to a comfortable warm rug. It was queer for I knew these rugs had been hanging on a line in the basement. While I wondered I heard a chuckle from the porch of a downstair flat.

"David did it," laughed my tenant. "I watched him. The chained dogs got restive in the wet. David went up to Adam. I saw him regard the chained pup. He then went to Eve, snuffed at her wet coat and turned back into the basement. Next thing I saw was David dragging the rug to Adam who lay down upon it. Then he went back and fetched the other rug for Eve. That David is uncanny!"

Yet for all David's wisdom Adam was the dominant character of the two. Both dogs possessed admirable traits for a kennel sire. I could not decide which to keep. At last the day came—the thing had to be faced.

I built a crate and furnished it with food and water. I took the buyer's letter from my pocket; my hand trembled as I printed the man's name on the crate. I did not know which dog was going, which one would stay. I read the letter again; either pup would meet the man's requirements —"Young, healthy, well-bred."

I leant over the gate watching the dogs at play in the

field. David saw me, came, snuffed at my trouble through the bars, thrust a loving tongue out to lick joy back into me.

"David, I cannot let you go!"

"Adam," I called, "Adam!" But my voice was low, uncertain.

Adam was romping with Eve and did not heed.

Common sense came hanging over the gate beside me and, looking through my eyes, said, "David is of Punk's siring. Adam's new blood would be best for the kennel." My face sank, buried itself in David's wool.

"Dog ready?" The Express Company's van was at the gate. The man waited to lift the crate. The two loose boards, the hammer, the nails were ready, everything was ready, everything but my decision.

"Hurry! We have that boat to make!"

I opened the field gate. David rushed through, jumped into the crate. I nailed the loose boards over David. Adam still romped in the field with Eve.

"David! David!"

Loo

LOO REACHED me first, her motherliness, always on the alert to comfort anything, pup or human, that needed protection.

I had watched someone die that night. It was the month of February and a bitter freeze-up—ground white and hard, trees brittle. The sick woman had finished with seeing, hearing and knowing; she had breathed laboriously. In the middle of the night she had died, stopped living as a blown-out candle stops flaming. With professional calm the nurse had closed her eyes and mouth as if they had been the doors of an empty cupboard.

When it was nearly dawn I went through bitter cold and half-light back to my apartment-house. It was too early to let the Bobbies out, but I wanted the comfort of them so I freed them into the garden, accepting their loving. Warmth and cosiness sprang from the pens when I opened the doors, then I went to tend my furnace. As I stooped to shovel coal, a man's heavy hand struck me across the face. A tenant living in one of my flats bellowed over me, "I'll teach you to let my pipes freeze!"

The shovel clanked from my hand—I reeled, fell on the coal pile. I had not seen the man follow me into the basement. Before I righted myself the man was gone, leaving the basement door open. Icy wind poured in. I sprang to slam the door, bolt the brute out. He was on the step, his hand lifted to strike me again. Quick as lightning I turned on the tap with hose attached at the basement door and directed the icy water full into his face; it washed the spectacles from his nose. Too choked, too furious, too wet even to roar, he turned and raced to his flat upstairs. I waited for his door to shut, then I ran into the garden, ran to the Bobbies.

The eagerness of Loo's rush to help me knocked me down. I did not get up, but lay on the hard snow path, my smarting cheek against its cold. Loo stood over me wanting to lick my hurt. I struck at her for a clumsy brute—told her to go away. The amazed dog shrank back. Punk and the rest crowded round; Loo, shamed and pitiful, crept behind the lilac bush. When I saw her crestfallen, broken-hearted, peeping from behind the bush, great shame filled me. A bully had struck his landlady. I had struck Loo whom I loved; Loo, symbolizing motherliness, most nearly divine of all loves, who had rushed to comfort me.

"Loo! Loo!"

She came, her forgiving as wholehearted as her loving. I buried my face in her shaggy warmth, feeling unworthy, utterly unworthy.

"Work is breaking me, Loo!"

The dog licked my hands and face.

But the apartment-house must be run; it was my living. The kennel? . . . I had supplied the Bobtail market. For the present the kennel was but expense. Dusting the snow off myself I went up to the studio taking Punk and Loo with me. On the table lay an open letter. A kindly woman on a farm wanted a dog—"Mother Bobtail already bred," she wrote. Giving myself no time to think I quoted Loo. Loo's chin rested on my knee as I wrote. I dared not look below my pen. Soon Loo would have another family.

"The joy of Loo in her puppies will ease her strangeness," I told myself, but—"Loo, Loo, I love you."

Remorseful, bitter—I loathed the money when it came, hated the approving nods, the words "wise," "sensible," which people stuffed into my ears when they knew of my decision. I loathed myself, cursed the grind that broke me and took my dogs from me. Punk searched every corner for Loo. Most he searched my face.

Last of the Bobtails

LOO HAD been gone two days when a dowdy little woman came and held out a handful of small change.

"A guardian and companion for my daughter—delicate, city-bred, marrying a rancher on a lonely island. She dreads the loneliness while her husband is out clearing his land. I thought a sheep-dog. . ."

The price was not that of half a pup. She saw how young my puppies were and began to snivel. "It will be so long before they are protective!"

I took her small money in exchange for Punk, took it to buy value for him in her eyes. Those meagre savings meant as much to her as a big price meant to a rich person. A dog given free is not a dog valued, so I accepted her pittance.

Loo gone, Punk gone—emptying the kennel was numbness. I let every dog go—all except Adam. I would keep just one. Their going gave me more leisure, but it did not heal me. I took young Adam and went to the Okanagan to try high air. I struck a "flu" epidemic and lay six weeks very ill in Kelowna.

They were good to Adam. He was allowed to lie beside my bed. At last we took the lake boat going to Penticton to catch the Vancouver train. The train came roaring into the station and the platform shook. Adam, unused to trains, bolted. In a jiffy he was but a speck heading for the benches above Penticton.

The station master took Adam's chain and ticket.

"Hi, Bill!" he called to a taxi-driver, "Scoot like hell! Overtake that dog. Put him aboard at the water tank two miles down the line. You can make it easy!"

At the tank no Adam was put aboard. I was forced to go

on alone. I wired, wrote, advertised. All answers were the same. Adam was seen here and there, but allowed no one to come near him. A shaggy form growing gaunter ever gaunter slunk through the empty streets of Penticton at night, haunting wharf and station. Everyone knew his story, people put out food. Everyone was afraid to try catching him. At great distances a lost terrified dog with tossing coat was seen tearing across country. It was hopeless for me to go up. No one could tell me in what direction to search. Then for months no one saw him. I hoped that he was dead. Two winters and one summer passed—I got a letter from a woman. She said, "We moved into a house some miles out of Penticton. It had been empty for a long while. We were startled to see a large shaggy animal dart from under the house. 'Adam!' I cried, 'Adam!' for I knew about the dog. He halted and looked back one second, then on, on, a mad terrified rush to get away from humans. There was a great hole under our house hollowed to fit his body," said the woman.

At night she put out food. She heard the dog snuff at the door crack. She did not alarm him by opening the door or by calling out. Adam was known the country over as "the wild dog."

One day the woman worked in her garden; something touched her. Adam was there, holding his great paw up. She wrote me, "Come and get him." But before I could start, a wire came saying, "Adam shipped."

I went into the Victoria freight shed. The tired dog was stretched in sleep.

"Adam!"

He quivered but he did not open his eyes.

"Adam!"

His nose stretched to my shoe, to my skirt—sniffing.

"Adam!"

One bound! Forepaws planted one on each of my shoulders, his tongue reaching for my face.

Everyone said, "Adam will be wild, impossible after nineteen months of freedom."

He had forgotten nothing, had acquired no evil habit. Only one torment possessed Adam—fear of ever letting me out of his sight again—Adam, the last of my Bobtails.